If I'm Diapering a Watermelon, Then Where'd I Leave the Baby?

Help for the Highly Distractible Mom

If I'm Diapering a Watermelon, Then Where'd I Leave the Baby?

Help for the Highly Distractible Mom

Carol Barnier

Emerald Books
P.O. Box 635
Lynnwood, WA 98046

Emerald Books are distributed through YWAM Publishing. For a full list of titles, visit our website at www.ywampublishing.com or call 1-800-922-2143.

If I'm Diapering a Watermelon, Then Where'd I Leave the Baby?
Help for the Highly Distractible Mom

10 09 08 07 06 05 04   10 9 8 7 6 5 4 3 2 1

Published by Emerald Books
P.O. Box 635
Lynnwood, Washington 98046

Library of Congress Cataloging-in-Publication Data

Barnier, Carol, 1960–
 If I'm diapering a watermelon, then where'd I leave the baby? : help for the highly distractible mom / by Carol Barnier.
    p. cm.
  ISBN 1-932096-13-2
 1. Home economics. 2. Mothers—Time management. 3. Home schooling. I. Title.
  TX147.B29 2004
  640—dc22

                    2004002899

ISBN 1-932096-13-2

Printed in the United States of America.

To my ever-supportive husband,
who years ago learned to love the "Mary" in me.

Acknowledgments

Special thanks are due to a number of people for their contributions to this book:

Several friends loaned their eyes, ideas, and encouragement in the early stages of this book, most especially my track buddies, Caroline and Sue, and my friend for a millennium, Mag. My father, grammarian extraordinaire, also loaned me his considerable editing skills toward the final product. Finally, I wish to thank Gina, who coined the phrase "La Di Da" to describe the carefree approach to which we both so greatly aspire.

Contents

I'm One of You

I recall years ago telling the women in my Bible study group something funny that my husband had said. I had found his comment to be so preposterous, so utterly ridiculous and laughable, that I just had to tell someone else. He had said I seemed to be moving at such a rapid and frenzied pace that he truly feared one day I would set the baby carrier down in the grocery store, put a melon in the cart, and walk blissfully, without baby, down the next aisle. I looked at him flabbergasted, wondering if he'd accidentally set his laser printer to stun. Didn't he understand that mother-baby bond?

So I gleefully started telling this amusing tale to my buddies and rolled my eyes as if to underscore the obvious idiocy of his comment. But then I suddenly had to stop talking. The women weren't laughing. I suddenly grew silent. I knew I had said something wrong, something uncomfortable. I hadn't been back in the faith for that many years. Perhaps it had become taboo in the church to say anything in amusement at the expense of one's husband. I saw that the women's heads were slightly downcast in embarrassment. No one was moving. But everyone's eyes were searching back and forth among the other faces in our circle, and finally, almost as a group, heads began nodding and comments began flowing forth. "Yeah…I could see *me* doing that." "Yeah, me too," admitted another, and another. One even confessed that she had pretty much done just what my husband had suggested. I sat there wide-eyed and speechless. How could this be? These women seemed to have it all together. Were my children the only ones *not* at risk of being left in the chilled fruit section of the grocery?

That was long ago, with my very first child. If you knew me today, I could fully trust that you would now be laughing out loud at my own naivete. Indeed, there are few women alive who have so completely missed the mark of perfect parenting as have I. I will admit, I had not yet come to grips with the reality of long-term parenting. I was fairly new. I was quite assured. In fact, my ignorance was only superseded by my arrogance.

It's not that my brain has become empty. On the contrary, it's that it has become overwhelmingly full.

Little did I realize just how well I would fulfill my husband's worst fears many times over. Little did I realize that the day would come when a visiting friend would open my cupboard, remove the gallon of now-warm milk, and ask me why it was in the cupboard, next to the bowls, in the first place. Without a smidgen of embarrassment, I was now suddenly able to recall where I'd left the stack of plates, now thoroughly chilled. Little did I realize that the level of exhaustion that accompanies a newborn could actually prompt me to absentmindedly throw a full, soiled, disposable diaper in the wash with the next load of clothes. (Am I oversharing here?)

It's not that my brain has become empty. On the contrary, it's that it has become overwhelmingly full. Nor is it my whole brain that is full but rather a very small, lower-functioning, maintenance-related portion of it. This is the brain area that allows moms the world over to simultaneously

- grab a kitchen towel from off her shoulder to wipe up the just-spilled juice while
- deftly sliding the school books out of the way of the ever-spreading puddle while
- leveling the tipping plate of cream corn being carried to the table by her three-year-old while
- over her other shoulder, informing her thirteen-year-old of the location of the much-sought shoe that matches the one dangling from the teenager's limp hand while
- casually mentioning that someone has left the bath water running upstairs while
- sliding the glass door open, without looking, to allow the approaching dog to enter while
- pushing the cereal crumbs more centrally *under* the middle of the table so they won't be tracked all over the house before they are vacuumed, all the while
- jiggling a baby non-stop on her hip.

Did you notice that nowhere in the midst of this onslaught is this mother ever asked to ponder any great philosophical questions? She isn't asked to give thoughtful commentary on the latest crisis in the news. And no one asks her to spend a few hours alone creating the lyrics for a great hymn or sonnet to transport and inspire our souls. Like me, this woman is very, very busy. But our busyness will most likely not land us the Nobel Prize for any of our efforts.

My guess is that I'm using only about 10 percent of my brain, at best, but I'm using that 10 percent at 185 percent of its capability. This poor little portion of my grey matter is always being asked to put out more than it was designed for. And it is being asked to do so at a nonstop, incessant, seagulls-swarming-around-your-head kind of pace. Once on a visit to Sea World years ago, I was standing at the dolphin petting pool and preparing to feed this sweet and very worthwhile mammal. A curious dolphin had planted itself directly in front of me, our eyes were locked in a cross-species attempt at communication, my hand was outstretched with a tiny morsel of a peace offering. And WHOOSH! Out

> **I have come to the conclusion that it would be best to obtain a master's degree in multi-tasking before taking on a house full of children.**

of nowhere there were at least forty seagulls swarming around my head, swooping down on me for a piece! That's pretty much what it's like caring for lots of children. You're dealing with this one thing, and suddenly you're also dealing with this and this and this and this ALL AT ONCE. And oh yeah, you're still trying to feed the dolphin. I have come to the conclusion that it would be best to obtain a master's degree in multi-tasking before taking on a house full of children. And when you consider that in our family, we also homeschool, you quickly realize that our house is ALWAYS full of children. I haven't had a thought that emanated from above my brain stem in over eleven years.

I do vaguely recall, though, how my brain components are *supposed* to be utilized. The design for correct usage is still somewhat (albeit vaguely) familiar to me. This tiny maintenance section of my brain was designed to be asked to produce…yes…but then it should be given a resting period, a recharging period, if you will, while *other* portions of my brain are supposed to be exercised and stimulated and stretched and expanded. (Feel the burn.) And then finally, calmly, after the passage of some time, my maintenance center would be asked to produce once again. But that pace and mix of proper brain uses belong to people of another world—people who get to go off into rooms and close the door.

Closed doors. Do you remember those? They're those rectangular things that hang on hinges between the bathroom and the rest of the house. You've probably forgotten what they look like, because even if you did manage to close the door upon entering the bathroom, you can count to no more than eight before the door is reopened by a creature with a question on the location of play dough or the fairness of his sister's division of the donut, or simply with a need to oust you so that he may partake of the facilities himself.

But back to the rest of the world. There are people who actually go into an office or even a cubicle to do their work, AND they get to do it without three thousand maintenance-related requests per hour. Now sometimes these people—husbands, friends, family—think their days are comparable to mine. They believe that because the phone rang, let's say six times in the last hour, that they can somehow "feel your pain," that they have a great understanding of just what we moms mean here. I don't buy it. Unless their job is playing eight ping pong matches at once, they don't feel *my* pain. Getting to complete one thought per fifteen-minute period is an extraordinary luxury. I had no idea the value of a completed thought until I was no longer permitted any.

This is not a book written by one of those women who is naturally organized, sort of a hybrid of Martha Stewart and the Proverbs 31 woman.

When I wrote my first book, *How to Get Your Child off the Refrigerator and on to Learning,* I spoke on that topic around the country at conferences and on radio talk shows. I presented ideas on how to keep unfocused children on task, how to keep highly distractible children moving forward with their schoolwork, and, above all, how to see these children, challenges and all, for the extraordinary gifts that they are. For each hour of actual public speaking, I got to spend dozens more speaking with moms and dads one-on-one. Over and over again I heard the question, "Forget about my kid. Where's the book for highly distractible moms?" At first I thought it was just a successful use of humor, because everyone around us laughed. But soon I began to see the real pain in the eyes of the asker.

- The real pain for that working mom who regularly misplaces important documents, loses her keys, or angrily calls roadside service to the house yet again to jump the car battery because some interior light was left on the night before.
- The real pain for the homeschooling mom who worries that her lack of organization is leaving growing gaps in her precious children's education. The pain of failure over math that doesn't get corrected regularly and, when it finally does, Mom now discovers that her child hasn't understood a vital concept for the past five weeks.
- The real pain of despair for any mom who realizes that her day saw twenty-seven projects started but only two that ever made it to completion—or maybe none.
- The pain and anger that eats at a woman's self-image when her disordered house seems to swallow, yet again, important schoolwork, or a book that was set aside for a much-anticipated study, or overdue library books.

- The weariness of being late to yet another event because she just can't seem to get everyone and everything together and out of the house on time.

It is for these moms that I write this book, for in all their questions and all their worries, I see and hear myself. No kidding. This is not a book written by one of those women who is naturally organized, sort of a hybrid of Martha Stewart and the Proverbs 31 woman. I've read those books. I've listened in awe as they pontificate about the lovely order and peace that reign in their homes. And I've felt the sting of judgment when I sense their utter amazement that I ever let myself get that disorganized in the first place. No, no, none of that here. I want you to know that I come to you as one of you. I'm every bit the highly distractible mom you might be, if not more so. I am the one who starts out to get her child a drink of water, stops briefly to pick up a paper clip from the floor, and ends up weeding in the garden with absolutely no understanding of why that child is still thirsty.

And yet, for all the ways I can name in which I've failed at providing a steady and consistent and highly organized home environment and educational structure for my children, *amazingly* they have survived. Indeed, they have really flourished in our home and our homeschool.

And I'll tell you something else…I think we gloriously unregimented moms (Don't you like that? It sounds so much better than "highly distractible.") have an edge that the highly organized mom doesn't have. Now, she *does* have some benefits. I won't take that from her. But we have some too. In my first book I wrote about the importance of not missing the gift in your child. But in this book I want to be sure that you haven't missed the gift in you. You may well be operating under the impression that highly organized women are superior to you and that you are somehow defective. But I'm here to tell you that YOU, just as you are, are a gift to your family, in ways that those structured and orderly women could never be. I'm not interested in turning you into a carbon copy of these lovely and naturally ordered moms. To do so would be to lose some of your very best strengths. Throughout this book, we will discover and develop a few tools to keep chaos at bay, but we will also discover ways of developing some of your strongest qualities—qualities that perhaps until now you've seen as weaknesses. Before we're done, I hope you've turned on the light of delight that I believe resides in you. Stick around. In the last chapter you'll discover what *you* have

Throughout this book, we will discover and develop a few tools to keep chaos at bay, but we will also discover ways of developing some of your strongest qualities—qualities that perhaps until now you've seen as weaknesses.

that makes you such a great asset and prize to your family. You'll learn the role that God designed you for. And you'll discover the quality you possess that sometimes leaves those highly organized women longing for the gift your personality style can provide.

What I hope to do here is to challenge you to look at things and at yourself a bit differently. Those highly organized women of the world are applauded and stroked so frequently that we often come away believing that what they are is the best way to be. They get attention. They get promoted. They get glowing praise in church circles, business circles, and even plain old mom circles. But what if this woman's gift is not your own? What if you spend so much time trying to make it *look* as if this is your gift that you never, ever see the gifts that you *do* have? At best, you could be a second-rate wanna-be, but then you'd never find the fully gifted, top-notch, delightful you that God designed you to be.

I want us to look ourselves squarely in the eye, see exactly who we are, see the beauty that comes from being a gloriously unregimented mom. I also want us to accept and own the truths, the very real challenges that come with our distractibility, instead of pretending that they shouldn't be there. You'll notice I didn't say to accept the ugly truths, because they aren't ugly. They're simply actionable truths. I call them Awareness Statements, and you really can work with them once you admit they're there. And the good news is, once you take on these truths about yourself, once you develop strategies to accommodate them,

life

gets

better,

because then and only then will you really accept yourself as the wonderful person that you already are.

Chapter 1

Awareness Statement #1:

We Will Forget

 **As gloriously unregimented moms,** we must admit that we *will* forget. You must begin by simply letting go of the idea that if you just

- were better organized,
- or were more at peace,
- or tried a little harder,
- or were a better person,
- or spent more time in prayer,
- or adopted a low-carb, high-insect diet,

you would start remembering things. Give it up. Whatever the reason for your lapses, it's gone. If you feel so inclined to have a reason, count your children. Each one removed one-third of your brain's ability to store and retrieve information. If you've had more than three…well…you do the math (if you still can!) Let's look at some strategies that you can use to successfully accommodate this newfound truth.

Borrow a Brain

I recently volunteered in our church nursery to help with an upcoming high-attendance day. I warned the staffing coordinator that there was only one teeny-weeny little problem. I knew with absolute certainty that when the day arrived for me to show up and actually work in the nursery, it could be guaranteed that I would have forgotten. This new mom smiled and said, "I understand. Isn't that just awful when you know there's something you're supposed to be doing and it just nags at you and nags at you…and it takes forever for you to remember it?" I looked at her with what I think was a pained expression and said, "Before I was forty, that was my experience, too. What you just said? That was it! But now…it doesn't even nag at me. It's just gone!" The woman informed me that she makes reminder calls, and that fixed that. I accepted that I would forget, and we arrived at a solution. I depended on something other than my brain to remember what I knew I would not.

I have discovered that I often turn for assistance to others whose brains store information more effectively than my own. Indeed, in writing this book I had just such an experience. I struggled with the precise wording for the specific concept of things that we needed to face. I finally came upon the plain and simple "Awareness Statement." I liked it because it implied no judgment. It was not a good thing if you had this quality. Nor was it a bad thing. It was neutral and simply a statement of fact about which you must be cognizant if ever you are to act upon it. However, at the exact moment in which I discovered this perfect phrase, I happened to be engaged in another activity. Quickly I turned to my son and asked him to remember my phrase as my mind was otherwise engaged, and I knew, again with absolute certainty, that the phrase would be gone when my current activity was finished.

> **When there is a pause in the conversation, I will no longer have any idea why I'm standing there.**

In retrospect, I know what happened next. My son thought, "Awareness Statement… "A" "S," okay, "A, S, A, S, A, S," and so it went. We both went back to our work. Several moments later, when my task was finished, I asked my son to resurrect this phrase from the sure and safe recesses of his superior and youthful brain. My fingers poised on the computer keyboard, anxiously waiting. Pause. Pause. I turned expectantly to look at him. Longer pause. His face began to contort. His hands twisted in the air as he grappled through the semisolid barrel of gelatin in which he mentally groped for the lost phrase. Finally, with great purpose and clear diction, he makes the pronouncement (I'm not making this up) "antelope stench." If there is anything to be learned from this, it's that the selection of an individual to be your temporary brain storage is a vital decision and must be rendered with great caution.

But back to the real value of the story, which is, if we can own the fact that we will forget, we will take steps to keep the information somewhere other than in our brains. In fact, that is the theme of my strategies. Take the information out of your brain and put it in a place where you can get to it. Almost *anywhere* will be more reliable than in our brains.

Tools That Free Up Brain Space

Since we've released ourselves from the idea that we're supposed to make our brains hold everything, we are now free to enthusiastically incorporate some useful tools into our bag of strategies.

Hand Cues

Here's a real simple one. I walk up to two women who are talking. I know I must wait for a pause in the conversation before I can ask my question. Common courtesy, right? But I also know that when there is a pause in the conversation, I will no longer have any idea why I'm standing there. So I developed a system that can work without my brain. In our family we have a deaf uncle; thus we have spent a great deal of time learning sign language and the sign language alphabet. One day I realized that if I just signed a letter of the alphabet and held it in my hand while the women talked, when they were done, the letter would cue me in on what I had wanted to ask. In other words, if I wanted to ask about the date of an upcoming picnic, I would choose a letter—probably "p" in this case—and simply hold it in my hand while I waited. The system doesn't require that my brain hold the information. My hand does it for me. (If you're not already familiar with the sign language alphabet, it's easy to learn. See the back of this book for a handy guide.)

> **My thought has a shelf life of perhaps one-eighth of a second before it bursts into nothingness.**

I also use this trick when I'm on the phone to help me hold onto my thought until an appropriate time presents itself. In the past I have had the really nasty habit of cutting people off in mid-sentence. I don't like this about myself or others and believe that this behavior often marks a particular kind of arrogance. But in my case, it really marks an awareness that my thought has a shelf life of perhaps one-eighth of a second before it bursts into nothingness, leaving only a misty vagueness that anything had ever been there at all. So again, in my hand I'll hold a letter that will prompt me later as to my thought. Thus, my thought and my manners remain intact.

One more application: Have you ever headed into another room to retrieve something but when you got there, you just stopped…and stood…and you *knew* you were there for a purpose but no longer had a clue what it was? Now, before I even head into the room, I anchor my thought in my hand, and I'm golden. Use the hand—it's everywhere you want to be.

Timers

Let's look at another tool for holding information that we are certain to forget if we leave it in our brains: timers. They're invaluable. Let's say you've finally got all your children sitting down together doing their schoolwork. Your son says, "Can I run upstairs and get my math book?" "Sure!!" you answer. That's a legitimate reason to leave the monitored work area. Off he runs. Time passes. You're enjoying the moment…there's something… hmmm…different about it. More time passes. You finally get the kitchen wiped down. More time passes. What is that pleasant something you're feeling? Wait a minute. It's…it's…no, wait…I'll get it in a minute. It's quiet! Where is that boy? Fifty-three minutes have now passed. If your child is also distractible, guess what he did? He ran upstairs and into his room…and then stopped…and then stood there…and he *knew* he was there for a purpose…and then he saw his pile of Legos.

> **If I'm foolish enough to think I should put something on my back burner, that something will leap off the back of the stove before I can even set the dial to simmer.**

Here's where timers come in. Although good timers aren't particularly cheap, get yourself as many as you can afford. Consider it an investment. Then, when one of your children wants to leave your jurisdiction, you say, "How long should that take you if you really stay on task?" You set the timer on your oven or microwave or wherever and then—here's the key—you attach another timer TO YOUR CHILD with the understanding that only YOU may remove it. This is so that when your timer goes off, you don't have the added task of going to find your child. He's had a reminder as well, and it's time for him to come back.

Assignments You Can Wear

I often give my children simple instructions like "Straighten up the shoes by the door" or "Carry your laundry upstairs." Here's the problem. I tell them to do it knowing full well that I'll need to check up on them later to see that the task was done. I mentally put it on my back burner. Okay. What's wrong this picture? That's right! I no longer have a back burner!

I *used* to have a back burner. Really, I did. I used to be able to say to people, "I'm going to put that on the back burner for awhile," or, "I've had that on my back burner for quite some time, and now I'm ready to do something about it." But at this point in my life, if I'm foolish enough to think I should put something on my back burner, that something will leap off the back of the stove before I can even set the dial to simmer.

So, back to my children and their assignments. I can't always remember all the things I've asked them to do. And they know (the little scamps) that if they just postpone doing the task for the teensiest bit of time, I'll forget. So when I discover that I am telling them to do something for a second time, I give them an assignment they can wear. I make a sash of party crepe paper that goes over the shoulder and around the child. On the sash I write the

child's assignment. This system actually helps my children, too, since they are just as likely as I am to forget their assignment. When they have completed the task, they must return to me because the sash can't come off until I know the job is done. Since they want this sash off, it tends to give them an incentive to do the job immediately. Also, their coming back to me allows me to check it off my list, thus

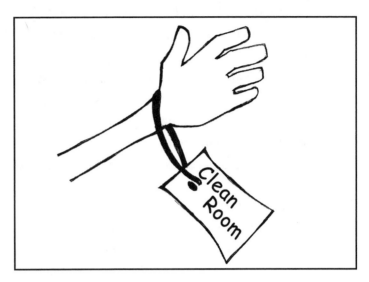

freeing my few remaining brain cells (already on an endangered list) from the nagging worry about whether or not the task was ever completed.

I found over time that I was consuming a lot of crepe paper, so I created wrist reminders. Same principle. I covered a 2 x 10-inch piece of paper with clear tape so that I could write on it with an erasable pen. This way it could be used over and over. I put a hole in one end and attached a soft, circular, stretchy hair band through the hole using a slip-knot. The length of the paper makes it a nuisance to wear. Thus, again the incentive is to quickly get to the task so as to be allowed the freedom of wrist-reminder removal. The plus to this version is that it is reusable, and you won't go through roll after roll of crepe paper. The downside is that there *is* a special delight for the child in dramatically ripping off the aforementioned sash when Mom's approval of the task has been granted.

Writing It Down...(duh)

My pastor told a story in one of his sermons about an older couple who find that they're forgetting much more than they used to. It really begins to be a problem. In fact, it bothers them so much that they go to see a doctor. After a thorough examination, the doctor says, "Stop worrying. There's nothing really wrong. You're just getting older. It comes with the territory. You simply need to start writing things down."

The couple heads home, and later that night they're watching TV together. Husband gets up and heads toward the kitchen. Wife says, "While you're there, get me some ice cream." He says, "OK," and keeps walking. She says, "I think you'd better write this down. Remember what the doctor said." He grumbles, "I don't need to write this down. You want ice cream. Got it!" "But I want it to be vanilla," she adds, "and I want some chocolate sauce.

And I also want one—no, maybe two—cherries on top of it. Please write this down." "I'm NOT writing this down. Vanilla ice cream…chocolate sauce…two cherries…no problem." Off he goes. He's gone a good twenty minutes. He comes back and hands a small plate to his wife. She looks down and sees bacon and eggs. She looks at the plate. And looks at him. She looks at the plate. Now she's clearly disgusted. "I TOLD you to write this down. Where is my toast!?"

This story resonates well with me because I am that couple *now*…and eighty is a long way off. So, long before my doctor suggests it, I'm developing the habit of writing it down. The tool of writing it down may seem too obvious and too easy. Or perhaps you're thinking, "Yeah, I can write it down, but I'll lose the little piece of paper." Don't be too quick to dismiss this. Let's look at some ways to make this tool—a really vital tool—work for us.

Borrowing and Loaning Books

You'll find I have a number of systems on borrowing and loaning books because I have a lot, I use a lot, I loan a lot, and I borrow a lot. I love to loan books. If I have a book I like, I really enjoy sharing it. Loaning books is so much more than simply loaning a gardening tool or handing off a cup of sugar. It's sharing an experience or a feeling or a meaningful insight. Some books have a real special place in my heart. And sharing part of that place is something I love to do. But often, without any malice or ill will on the part of the borrower, the books don't find their way back home. If people see a book lying around their house long enough, the book begins to look familiar, and soon they think of it as just one more of their own books. So on your bookshelves, in a well-chosen and consistent place, you must keep a ledger.

> **Often, without any malice or ill will on the part of the borrower, the books don't find their way back home.**

1. Write your name in the cover of the book.
2. Write the title of the book loaned, the date it was loaned, and TO WHOM it was loaned in your ledger, which goes right back on the shelf in that well-chosen and consistent place.
3. Every so often, check back in the ledger and make a note of books that have made it back home. Occasionally I'll "call back" all my wayward books, checking with the borrowers to see whether they still truly need to have the book in their possession.

Now let's cross over to when YOU are borrowing a book. I'm just as susceptible as anyone to sort of absorb someone else's book and come to think of it as my own. So when I borrow a book, I slide a strip of brightly colored paper, like a sleeve, onto the cover of the book. I write on this strip the name of the person from whom the book was borrowed and when. So now, when the book is lying about my house, as books do that are currently being read, I can never forget that it's not mine. That brightly colored strip of paper is a constant reminder that this is someone else's property. I've also learned over time to leave a long flap at the end of the circular strip which then serves as a handy bookmark while I'm reading the book.

Dial-a-Child

Our kids rotate certain chores in our house. We used to assign whole days to different kids. Monday was laundry-folding day for this child, Tuesday went to another child…and so on. The problem was that I might go days without doing any laundry and then do ten loads in one day, which then meant that one child gets an unfair share of the work. So my kids said they'd really like to rotate on each load. Great! That seemed fair. But of course, it required that I remember who did it last. Or worse yet, the children had to remember, and of course the incentive is quite high to remember that it's your sibling's turn and not yours. So I created the laundry dial. It's a simple reminder with a moveable arrow that points to whichever child is up next for folding duty. Now when the laundry buzzer goes off, I check to see which child is up next and call that child in. When the child has folded the laundry, he or she flips the dial. If the dial doesn't get flipped, guess what? The same child has to do the next load. I will not assume the role of mediator if the child doesn't perform that simple task. How many times do you suppose they have forgotten to flip? Just once.

Laundry Tips

While we're on the subject of laundry, let me share another tip that frees up loads of time. Once, a few years back, I paused to actually observe what I was doing when I did the laundry. See if this sounds even remotely familiar. I went into each bedroom and gathered the dirty laundry (touched it once). I took it downstairs to sort it (touched it a second time). I put a load in the wash (now we're on the third touch). I moved it to the dryer (fourth). I took each item from the dryer, folded it, and put it into a hamper (fifth). I picked up and carried the whole kit and caboodle (sixth) up the stairs to my nice, big flat bed, whereupon I sorted every item into piles representing each family member (seventh) and then took each pile to the bedroom of the appropriate person (eighth). I knew there had to be a better way. I tried to think like those time-efficiency experts hired by fast-food restaurants when they streamline the movements of employees behind the counter. I knew that one important objective was to minimize my number of "touches."

> **I tried to think like those time-efficiency experts hired by fast-food restaurants.**

The first task was to get my kids in the regular habit of grabbing their laundry as they come down the stairs first thing in the morning. They're already making the trip. Why not have their hands full? Second, they had to put the laundry down in the laundry area. So if they're going to put it down, why not put it down in piles separated by color? (Although I'm describing this little habit in just a few sentences, in reality this initial step took many weeks to accomplish. Unlearning old habits takes much time and patience. Be kind.)

Then it was my turn. Certainly I had to put the clothes into the washer and then into the dryer (although I did ponder a few engineering marvels by which the washer would rise mechanically on a hoist and tip sideways, dropping the clothes in a simple pile on the outstretched lid, which then shut itself. But back to reality.)

The biggest change for me came when I realized that I could sort right out of the dryer. I skipped the community hamper in which I had previously placed all folded laundry and instead put up a sort of cubby or shelf by the dryer. The clothes are now folded straight out of the dryer, put in the section bearing the name of wearer, and I'm done. This saves many steps over the usual in-the-basket, to-the-bed, sort-and-deliver system. All children are responsible for getting their clothes from their cubby to their rooms. This was the other end of the habit cycle for my newly trained children. Just as they had to bring down their dirty laundry each morning, they had to learn to take up their now clean laundry as they went to bed each night. They're going there anyway, they might as well have something in their arms.

Learn to Love Labels

If it doesn't move, LABEL IT. Here's how I used to think in my prelabeling days. I would one day, in disgust, decide to organize, say, my pantry. All the cereals and grains in one area, baking products in another, and so on. When I was done, it was a thing of beauty. An artwork of form and function. I just *knew* that when my children next put something away, they would naturally follow such a clear and obvious system. Which just shows how many fries short of a Happy Meal I can sometimes be. Of *course* they didn't follow the system. What system? They thought the system was "Is there an open spot anywhere on any shelf? Yes…then that's where this goes." What's worse, I hadn't yet come to grips with the truth that as a gloriously unregimented mom, *I* wouldn't remember where things go. So the next obvious step was to label everything. Once I had created my extremely ordered pantry shelf of beauty, I put labels on the walls of each region or category. There was a region for tomato products, one for soups, one for grains and pastas, even an "Ethnic" area for my Chinese, Mexican, and Middle Eastern ingredients. I have a labeled box for sweet snacks and another for salty snacks. This system has been in place for three years and has really stood up quite well. No one has to think about where things go. The information is no longer held by anyone's brain. It's on the wall on little 3 x 5 cards with big, black letters.

> **If it doesn't move, LABEL IT.**

Here are some other things we've labeled in our house:

- My children's clothing drawers. In the past they'd shove anything anywhere and then couldn't find it when they needed it.
- My own clothing drawers.
- Closet rod. I put separators on the rod, just like you'd find in a department store. I cut donut-like circles from old, heavy, vinyl place mats and then wrote my headings on them. In my baby's closet I have a section for dresses, shirts, one-piece outfits, and jackets. All her shorts and pants are on the shelf above. I can actually see all her clothes at one time, making finding matches in the morning much easier than when everything was hidden away in drawers.
- Shelves. I have a shelf of math materials, one of science materials, and one of pre-school materials. Our little library is labeled: History, Poetry, Classics, Biographies, Fiction, Religion, Comedy, etc. When the children are finished with a book from our little library, they can place it into a big "Returns" box. Every so often we go through the box and reshelve the books. With the labels up, Abraham Lincoln's biography no longer gets lost for months among the Dr. Seuss books.
- The medicine pantry. We have a box of items for colds, one for mouth and tooth products, one for topical applications, one for stomach products, one for pain-related products, and one for medical instruments (thermometer, heating pad, tweezers, etc).
- Our huge collection of craft supplies and doodads.
- My children's cast-off clothing boxed up in the attic. I have boxes marked 2yr/Girl, 4yr/Boy, etc.

- Our science materials—one box each of shells, feathers, light and magnifying things, bones, magnets, rocks, seeds, and lots of bug stuff.

Labeling takes the guesswork out of sorting. The mind that has to stop and think often doesn't bother. So make it easy for everyone to follow your ordered system.

Wall Your Callbacks

There is nothing worse in my mind than having someone return my call and for me to have no idea who she is or why I called her in the first place. I now use posted call-back notes. Let me explain. If I request that someone call me back, I will write down the info on either a sticky note or even a scrap of paper. At the top of the paper, underlined, is simply the person's name. I put the paper on the wall by a specific phone, the same place every time. Now when the person calls back, the first thing I do is get her name, and then I follow up by saying "Oh, sure, thanks for calling. Can you hold while I switch phones?" Then I walk—usually still generally clueless as to who this person is—to my specific callback spot, look for that name, grab the note from the wall, and jump right into the call, fully conversant on the subject. The caller need never know the immense vacuum that took over my mind when first I heard her name.

Whose Toy Is It?

My children often have the lovely spirit of generosity. A sibling sees an object, asks if he might have it, and sometimes is greeted with the astounding statement that indeed he may! Either the giving child finds that she no longer has need of the item or she has outgrown her interest in it, the play factor is gone, she's moved on, or she's tired of keeping it tidy. Who knows. So she willingly—yes, even generously and with great fanfare—passes the object along. Now, fast-forward to some point in the future. This item again appears in discussion. But this time there is great argument over just who has true ownership. It starts with "That's mine." "No it's not." "Yes it is. You gave it to me." "No I didn't. I only loaned it to you." "No, you didn't" yada, yada ad nauseam (Yiddish Latin).

> I realize that my brain can do many wonderful things, but that holding on to short-term information is not one of them.

The solution is so very, very simple. Any item, when given, is not truly and legally given unless I am presented with a 3 x 5 card naming the giver, the givee, the given, and the date. I file these cards in my file cabinet in a file labeled "Gifts." There is no transfer of ownership without the card. If an argument ensues regarding a supposed transfer, I search for my card. No card, no new owner, no argument.

Piles of Prayers

I'm going to allow you a peek into my prayer life, a profound testament to God's patience. My prayers can easily and often do go like this:

> Dear Lord, please keep my son safe today as he travels back from his camping trip. Let the driver be rested, his eyes sharp, Ohhh…that reminds me, I need to make an eye appointment for Katie. She's holding her books way too close. I was surprised the library didn't have more books from that American Girls series. They're so popular. They must get a lot of use, too, 'cause they were lookin' pretty ratty. Wonder why they didn't cover them in that heavy plastic to protect them. There's an idea. I could use some of that on our books at home. No, I'm already out of shelf space, and that just makes the books fatter…ha! Just like me. Man! Jan and Ellen are sure looking great. But the letter "P" diet! I just can't get past that name. And parsnips, potatoes, and parsley has *got* to get old.

And on and on it can go. What little quiet time I have can be squandered away by my wandering mind. So I've taken to using prayer flash cards. I write each item I'm praying for on a 3 x 5 card. With it sitting in my hand, it's hard to get too far off track because I'm constantly peeking at my cue card. I work my way through the cards to be sure I've covered each family member, each friend, and each issue that I've felt the need to pray for. The serendipitous and unexpected perk to this system is that once a prayer has been answered, the card goes into my answered-prayers file. This has been a WONDERFUL place to return to every now and then to remind myself of the oft-forgotten provisions of God in my life.

> **What little quiet time I have can be squandered away by my wandering mind.**

Just My Size

In thinking about the ways that I've learned to accommodate my tendency to forget, I'm reminded of an incident years ago, when my husband and I were snorkeling. I use the words "my husband and I," but in fact *he* was snorkeling. I was doing my best to drown. And this in only four feet of water. Nonetheless, that water kept filling up my mask. My flippers kept slipping off. So when I found myself choking and sputtering, I couldn't even right myself to stand because the flippers stood straight on end, making me teeter forward and backward with the comings and goings of the waves. My beloved kept glancing over at me with this look of pity, clearly pained that he had joined his life to one so uncoordinated. I felt a failure. I couldn't even manage this simple activity that my husband adored.

Finally he realized I just wasn't going to get it. He came over and began to help me to shore. I couldn't have been more defeated. And then, bless his heart, he discovered that my mask and flippers were the wrong size. You'd think this might have occurred to me (or to him?). But it didn't because I was convinced that if I applied a set of tools to the job, the same tools I'd seen others use, they would work for me as they had for others. I had to acknowledge that I needed a set of tools made specifically for me. What a joy for me when I discovered that with a better "fit," I was as capable as the next person to bob as a cork in the water and not drown.

I have made the very same discovery when it comes to forgetting things. Instead of trying to use my brain to work for me in the same way other peoples' brains work for them, I accept that I am wired differently. I realize that my brain can do many wonderful things, but holding on to short-term information is not one of them.

Trying to hold information in brains like ours is like trying to catch the rain in a pillowcase. You might slow it down a bit, but no matter how hard you try, it's still going to drip out. Wouldn't you be better served by getting solid, reliable containers that do the job more effectively? And wouldn't it make sense to acknowledge this fact? When I freed my mind from trying to hold vast amounts of maintenance-related information, I felt as though I had mentally lost ninety pounds. I relished the greater calm inside my head as other tools took over for my weary and battle-worn brain cells. But best of all, I was no longer forgetting information that I needed.

Chapter 2

Awareness Statement #2:

We Will Lose Things

Just as we must accept the fact that we will forget things, in the very same vein, we will lose things. Physical items can be misplaced just as easily as mental items. Indeed, the main reason we lose something physical is because our mind can't recall where we last left it. So it's a continuation of an already established theme. And even if we could manage never to mislay another item, our children will happily fill the void. There are, thankfully, actions you can take, strategies you can use that will minimize some of the more repetitive and annoying search-and-find missions you regularly put yourself through.

Tie Me Kangaroo Down, Sport

One item I've been known to travel through thirteen rooms seeking is a simple pair of scissors. I would open and root through a dozen drawers and corners before finding this essential item. And by the following morning, when I needed them again, guess what? They weren't where I had left (or at least where I "thought" I may have left) them, and I had to begin my search anew. What a frustrating waste of time. When it first clicked with me that perhaps I should come up with a plan to end this almost daily ritual, my solution, in retrospect, was laughable. I decided that if I simply purchased additional scissors—say maybe eight pairs—there would certainly be a pair nearby when I needed them. As my college professor of logic would say, this is a false assumption. I soon realized that my strategy would need adjustment because my children will ferret away the various scissors available, whether I have two or twenty-two. So the most useful thing I learned was, if at all possible, tie it down…tether it…string it up to something that will not be moved.

Stop and ask yourself, what items do I waste time looking for over and over? Can they be tethered somewhere?

I have tied a pair of scissors and a stapler to a table leg near my desk. I made a little holster for the scissors out of heavy poster stock paper and attached it to the leg of the table. Then I tied the end of the string to the bottom of the holster, taping it so it wouldn't slide down the leg. A similar holster could easily be fashioned for the stapler. This keeps both items handy, yet avoids having them and their strings laying all over the table surface and becoming intertwined. In addition, I've taped down a tape dispenser. These items cannot become lost.

The other item which, when tethered, has improved the quality of my life is the simple hairbrush. We own approximately three hundred of them. But my daughter, who believes the combing of hair is unnatural at best and a torture at worst, can never seem to find even one as we head out the door. No more. Not only is there a brush tethered in a bathroom, but also I have one tethered in the van. If I miss my daughter before she exits the house, I'll get her in the car.

A few other things I've tethered over time:

- The white-board erasers are tied to some place close to the white boards.
- Tweezers are tethered to my make-up area.
- A pen is tethered to my wallet.
- A calculator is tethered to the area where I work on bills.

All this tethering can be done in many ways. The hairbrushes usually have a convenient hole in the handle. The tweezers may also have a handle on which you can tie your string. But if not, you can tape a piece of string onto your item and then knot the end of the string so that it won't slide out of the tape. If you'd like a cleaner look on the pen in your wallet, get one of those foam grips that kindergarten kids use to soften the grip on their pencils. Place it on your pen, sliding it right over a piece of string that you can then use to create a loop. One of the nicest gifts I ever received was a retractable string that a friend had purchased for me from a quilt shop. I can attach it to any of my smaller tethered items, and there is no inconvenient and grubby looking string flapping about. For heavier items, consider using a retractable laundry line.

And please remember that no tethered item should be located where young children could get to it; the tether could end up wrapped around their necks. Think carefully about where these anchored items can be safely attached.

So if you find yourself doing yet another ridiculous search and rescue, just stop and ask yourself, what items do I waste time looking for over and over? Can they be tethered somewhere? If they can, tie those puppies down.

Library Books

Library books can be the bane of every distractible mom's existence. We need the library. Can't get away from that. We want the library. It's full of wonderful resources that we don't want to go out and buy for ourselves. But here's the problem. You take all your children to the library on Library Day, and you come home with thirty or so books, which promptly go to the various four corners of your house. When it is time to gather the books up to return them, you have only twenty-two, and you have no idea exactly how many you had originally or what the titles of the missing books are. When we lived in Chicago, we were fortunate enough to belong to a library system that gave us a printed receipt of the books just checked out, including a due date for each book! Wonderful, although not all libraries provide this service.

The best solution I've ever heard of came in an article by Kathy Von Duyke in *Practical Homeschooling* magazine.[1] Before she even leaves the library, Kathy takes all the books to the copy machine, stacks them up, turns them spine-down onto the copier, and makes one copy of all the book titles at once. Isn't that smart? I wish I'd thought of it. Remember when you get home to post the copy on the wall. If you lay it on any horizontal surface, it is likely to go the way of things you've placed on your back burner.

While we're on the subject, here are two other great ideas that Kathy suggested for using a copy machine. No need for expensive matching games for your preschooler. Take a few everyday objects from around your house (key, paper clip, barrette, spoon) and make a quick copy. Then have your preschooler match the object to the image. How simple is that?

But here's my favorite. In previous plant studies in our house, we have gathered great specimens from our nature walks, carefully flattened them, waited weeks (read that months to years) for them to dry between the pages of blotting paper in a large, heavy book, mounted them oh so carefully, often damaging their fragile, paper-thin leaves, and then… then…then FINALLY, we got to label their parts. Of course by this point we'd forgotten the parts of the plant that we'd studied so many eons ago when we first began this project. Kathy's wonderful suggestion is to place the freshly gathered specimens on your copier and make copies. No waiting. No drying. No mounting. No copyright laws. And instant labeling opportunities with a crystal-clear plant sample.

For a full listing of Kathy's ideas for using copiers, check out the archived articles at www.home-school.com, the official website of *Practical Homeschooling* magazine.

A Home for Your Keys

You're trying to get everyone out the door. If you're to arrive on time, you should have left eight minutes ago. You've sent your kids upstairs three different times to get the needed item of clothing or homework or music that must go along on this trip. The diaper bag is in your hand. The kids have shoes on. They actually match. Now…grab your keys. Did you just pause? Do you know where your keys are? Always? How many times have you frantically raced through your house, shaking out purses, patting down coat pockets, lifting up couch cushions, seeking those constantly disappearing keys? Make a determination right now to never lose your keys again. Give them a specific home. As you exit your car and come into your house, what place do you pass *every single time?* We enter through the same door consistently, so at this door there is a table. (My sweet, departed, and very English Aunt Gladys used to call these tables "azyoo's" It was a table you passed "as you" went from here to there.) On our "azyoo" we've placed the designated key basket. We make it the "home" for all keys. You can't enter the house unless you drop your keys here. And you cannot leave the house without passing this basket on your way out. Make it convenient, and use it consistently.

Do you know where your keys are? Always?

Now, what do you do with your keys when you're getting out of the car in the parking lot of your destination? Do you shove them in a coat pocket? Maybe in a purse? Do you have a specific spot where you put them? If not, select one right now. I put a carabiner on my key ring. You may not know it by name, but you've certainly seen one before. It's one of those rings of metal with a hinged section that rock climbers use with their ropes. That hinged section allows me to rapidly and securely attach my keys to anything and then just as rapidly retrieve them. Since I carry a purse, they always, always, always are attached to the strap on my purse as I exit my car. Then when I return to my car, I no longer stand around in a dark parking lot, groping in every available key-sized space in search of my way to get into my car. Find your place of choice, a specific home for your keys. Then determine to use it so as to never lose them again.

Lost and Found Game Pieces

Assume that you'll lose game and puzzle pieces. Have a lost-pieces box stored in the same cupboard or shelf as the games and puzzles. Any stray piece, when found lying on the carpet, tucked between the cushions, or buried in a toy box, is put in this Lost and Found box. When the game is next played and a piece is discovered to be missing, check the box and chances are it's there.

Use Your Vertical Wall Space

On the inside of the kitchen cabinet, tape up a chores list for your kids to refer to. I also have a list of my kids' ten favorite meals to prompt my slow brain at dinnertime. By your phones, put up a list of often-called numbers. Keep the most commonly used addresses on the wall near your stamps. Don't forget that xeroxed copy of library book spines. The nicest thing about using the insides of cabinet doors is that it doesn't make your home look cluttered but still allows you to keep vital information handy.

Invest in Electronic Finders

Maybe it's car keys you often lose. Maybe it's glasses. Maybe it's your purse. Maybe the TV remote. Don't despair. Modern technology has the answer for you. They're called "Key Finders," but these devices find a lot more than keys. You simply attach the device to whatever you typically lose and then, when you press the button of a remote control kept elsewhere (tethered, of course), your missing item beeps loudly and blinks so you can find it even in the dark. I did a search on the web using the phrase "find your lost keys" and got a bunch of companies offering a variety of features and prices. Be forewarned. I also had an ominous-sounding hit from a group known as Pagan Path, which promised to not only help you divine the location of your keys but also aid you in making major life decisions. It is my hope that you can exercise discernment in your web searches.

You certainly can't prevent all losses. The dryer will continue to eat half of a pair of socks. It's a law. I think it's in Leviticus. But for many of us, the great majority of things that we lose are *the same things*…over and over again. We can minimize a large portion of these time-wasting searches by using just a few thought-out strategies.

Endnote

1. Kathy von Duyke, "Photocopying Ideas," *Practical Homeschooling Magazine*, #3, 1993.

Chapter 3

Awareness Statement #3:

We Must Limit Our Interruptions

Distractions bother everyone. But for we gloriously unregimented moms, they can spell disaster. If we get off task, we may never get back on and, at the end of the day, we may find that nothing on our to-do list can be marked off as done. Interruptions to our thoughts come from all sides. (Speaking of distractions, some day, for kicks and giggles, make a hash mark for each time the word "mom" is called in your house.) We need tools to minimize the number of interruptions we get. In addition we need to control the impact of the interruptions that are inevitable. Some serious strategies are called for here.

Children Interrupting Adults Talking

There was a time when children were never to interrupt two adults talking. Even if there were a break in the conversation, children were to remain silent. Seen and not heard was the expectation by all. That would not describe our family. Heard and seen and felt would be more like it. Besides, I am interested in what my children have to say. Likewise, there are times when they need my input if they are to accommodate my expressed directions for them. Generally speaking, interrupting me when I'm talking to another adult is not a problem. But *how* they interrupt can be.

From some friends of ours, we learned this method that allows children to respectfully let you know they need your input on something. It is a system children can use when Mom or Dad is talking with another adult. The child calmly comes up beside you, places his or her hand on your shoulder, and then…WAITS. When there is a convenient and appropriate place to pause in the conversation, you, the parent, turn to your child to hear what it is that he or she needs. Please note that the hand on the shoulder is to rest lightly and NOT to pump the shoulder as though drilling for oil. Once my children understood that delicate little nuance, this procedure worked quite well for us.

> **We need to teach our children discernment about what questions are interruption worthy.**

I have also asked my children to use this delightful little politeness practice when I'm typing on the computer, playing the piano, or talking on the phone. When I'm on the piano, it is almost painful for me to stop playing in the middle of a musical phrase. When I'm on the computer, if not permitted to complete my thought I will…well, you know where I'm headed. When I'm on the phone, I can take the time to politely let the person I'm speaking with know that I need to go. A gentle hand on my shoulder gives my brain the much-needed margin to make transitions with closure and grace.

Children Interrupting During a Phone Call

We've just covered *how* interruptions should occur when they indeed are going to occur. But a bigger question to address is, should they occur at all? We need to teach our children discernment about what questions are interruption worthy.

Have you ever called someone long distance, chatted happily for a time, but soon found you were spending your time (and your dime) listening to your friend trying to carry on a conversation but having to correct her interrupting children? Have you ever been a bit annoyed at that someone? Have you ever *been* that someone? While I find this behavior to be rude, I will also confess that sometimes I have engaged in it myself. For the sake of being polite to the person I'm speaking to, I truly prefer to be left alone while on the phone (not to mention that if my train of thought is derailed, it will never again find its way back to the station).

In our house an interruption of mom while she's on the phone is a punishable offense unless there is either a dirty diaper or an injury that has actually drawn blood. The punishment is usually something fairly innocuous, but it doesn't take much to train our kids that inconveniencing mom with an interruption means an inconvenience for them as well.

Children Arguing

One of the most annoying intrusions upon my tenuous thought streams is the arguments of my children. I used to always leave what I was doing, scramble quickly to the fracas, and attempt to referee. Indeed, sometimes this is an entirely appropriate response—say, when knives or flames or giant gaping wounds are involved. (Grossly overstated—It was more like a spark than a flame!) But sometimes, in lesser conflicts, I noticed that my involvement in a disagreement only served to stir the passions further. In fact, I concluded that sometimes the escalation of the argument was really more for my benefit than an actual attempt to engage the battling party. I came to realize that some arguments were really a sad attempt simply to get Mom's attention. So I invented…

> **I came to realize that some arguments were really a sad attempt simply to get Mom's attention.**

The Stink Room

The Stink Room is a place to which my children are sent when they "make a stink" in their conversation. Rather than let them pollute the room (and disrupt my thoughts) with their unpleasant exchanges, they must retire to this predetermined room. Ours is the laundry room. I shut the door. In this room they will find some paper, a pen, two stools placed at quite some distance from each other, and a Bible. With no Mom audience and no referee, they must resolve this conflict on their own. They must write out a resolution. They must both sign and date the agreed-upon resolution. They must find and mutually agree upon a Bible verse that applies to this situation and include it in their resolution. And finally they must present it to me. If I approve it, they're done. They may reenter the nonstinking world. But if the resolution is defective in any way, back they go. Round two.

The benefit of this system is that I am out of the process. I am no longer an audience to their attention-getting efforts. They soon learn that anything they wish to do, from schoolwork to play, reading to running, cannot even be attempted until they first fix this conflict in a satisfactory manner. It is in their best interest to resolve it and get on with life. Eventually that's what they do.

Monastery Day

Some days I wake up and things are truly lovely. The sun is coming up. The birds are providing an extemporaneous symphony, delivering it through my open windows. And every verbal greeting between family members is loving and kind and uplifting. There really are some days like that. I'm not trying to be sarcastic (for a change).

But then there are other days…

All of us can exhibit the very human behavior of being angry about one thing and taking it out on someone wholly unrelated to the anger. Certainly wrong. Certainly not godly. And regrettably, certainly common.

There have been some days in which one of my children can't seem to produce a single kind word from his or her mouth. My children are well acquainted with Ephesians 4:29: "Do not let any unwholesome talk come out of your mouth but only what is helpful for building others up, according to their need that it might benefit those who listen." I know they know better.

Just because I'm their mother, and just because I will love them no matter how they treat me, doesn't mean they have my permission to treat me badly.

I firmly believe that having someone who loves you is a privilege. It is a gift that should not be taken lightly and certainly should never be abused. There have been times when I have felt that my children have stepped over the line with each other or with me. They have taken for granted this person in their lives who loves them, day in and day out. If I did nothing in response to this, I would be teaching my children the unspoken and ugly lesson that it is permissible to use another person as their verbal punching bag. Just because I'm their mother, and just because I will love them no matter how they treat me, doesn't mean they have my permission to treat me badly.

On days such as these, I have been known to declare a Monastery Day. It becomes a no-speaking day. The privilege of being allowed to share your thoughts with someone who loves you is suspended because it has been abused. The few times I have used this corrective measure, the awareness of the value of this privilege was palpable. You could feel it in the air. You could hear it in the silence. You could see it on the faces of my children in the many number of times that they wanted to speak, to touch base, to obtain a thought or opinion, to share something funny that they'd just read, only to realize that they couldn't. It *was* a privilege. And it was gone.

Also on such days, the quiet eventually became a friend. While the usual fast-paced, ping-pong action of our conversations was missing, the peace that replaced it was lovely in a different way. The day was more thoughtful. Its pace was slower and restful. It was recuperative rather than exhilarating. And I am convinced that such quiet episodes also allow us to better hear the still, small voice of our Father. My children have never failed to be sincerely sorry for their previous unkind words. And sorry in a way that changed them. Maggie Erber, a homeschooling mom and speaker, says she makes time *each day* for her children to have a bit of silence. She says they need time every day in which the sound of life is simply turned off.

I have never maintained our Monastery Day for an entire day. In fact, it probably hasn't gone beyond a few hours. And for the sake of vital exchanges (school questions, permission requests), I did allow basic needs to be submitted in writing and then only if necessary. But in those few hours it has always been an experience for which I have been grateful. It's sort of an auditory version of what we feel when the electric power goes out. At first it's a real inconvenience and all you feel is annoyed. You have to dig out the candles. You can't open the fridge or turn on the stove. In our case, living in the country means the well won't even deliver up water. But as you find yourself hours later, the whole family sitting together by candlelight, sharing granola bars and listening to Dad read a story, you sort of get into the different pace of things and you find you're enjoying the emotional breather it provides. A period of silence can work the same wonders.

Off-Task Questions

Have you ever been in any group decision-making meeting (women's ministry committees, board meetings, support group planning sessions, PTAs) and found that one, seemingly innocent, off-task question took away the focus of the whole group for the next two hours? I've used a tool in working with my children that would be useful in any group that has difficulty staying on the agenda.

Here's how it plays out in our house when we're tightly focused on a school activity. I finally get Junior working on his spelling. All seems to be going well. A good forty-four seconds have passed, and then he presents the lofty question, "Mom, if ice were to sink instead of float, how would our lives be different?" I've been in church board meetings designed to cover the proposed building plans when someone asks, "When are we going to switch to real bread and ditch those little wafers?" I recently learned of a support group that took almost two years just to select a name for their group. Some questions can just absorb time like a sponge. Some questions are totally frivolous and, let's be honest, were put forth as an effort to delay (ever hear of a filibuster?) And yet, at other times they're really good. You could even use them as a launching point for excellent educational conversations and activities.

So we created a "Save It for Later" system. Sometimes it has been a spiral notebook. Sometimes it's a whiteboard. Doesn't matter. Just pick a place. If a thought crosses the mind of my children AND it is unrelated to the work they are currently engaged in, it must go in the Save It For Later spot. Each thought that they have must be evaluated. Is it worth the steps and the time to go record it? Is it worth the interruption to what they're presently engaged in? Many thoughts aren't. The child knows better and doesn't bother to go through the process. The blessing of this is that chances are, if the thought wasn't worth the interruption to them, it wasn't worth interrupting you either. But many thoughts *are* worth further discussion. When such a thought hits your child, the child can then take the time to go to the Save It For Later spot and jot it down. During break times, when answering these questions doesn't interrupt a focus-worthy task, you can go back to the Save It For Later spot and cover the items, which often make for great lunchtime or travel-time conversations.

Incoming Phone Calls That Interrupt

Does the phone *ever* ring at a convenient time? Am I *ever* able to keep my conversations short and to the point? I must admit, phone calls are a constant interruption to our day. I must also admit that tackling this particular interruption was really hard for me because I *need* to talk to other women. I *need* to connect with other human beings who aren't seeking my advice on how to spell the word *principal*. More than once I have turned to the phone for that connection. My kids have rightfully complained about phone calls making me inaccessible to them and thus putting them behind in their schedule. So at one point I just threw in the towel and stopped answering the phone.

Oh

my

goodness.

I couldn't believe how much smoother our days were, how much more I could keep my children and myself on track. It's probably the single best thing I ever did for taking control of the pace and peace in our school day.

Did I miss chatting with friends? Yes. But I also discovered that because our days went so much more smoothly and were infinitely less frustrating, my need to chat was lessened. I also learned to fill this gap somewhat by making a very natural transition to using e-mail more often. With e-mail I don't get off the subject and ramble on forever. I can send a letter when it fits into my schedule AND when I'm not stepping in on someone else's day. The people I write to can then check their e-mail at their convenience.

The phone had become more than just a tool that I use; it had begun using me.

I'll be honest. It was truly painful at first to just let that phone ring. I would hear that familiar ring, and I would pivot my head toward the phone, staring at it hypnotized. This battle would begin in my brain. Do I stay in my seat? Do I bolt for the phone? What if the police are calling to say a loved one has been in an accident? What if, what if, what if! It caused very real angst in me. Eventually, however, that angst made me realize that the phone had become more than just a tool that I use; it had begun using me. It was wonderfully freeing to learn to just let it ring. If a friend had called while I had been out on errands, they would have been unable to speak to me directly. People understand that you have other things to do and may not be available. Well, I can have other things to do even while in my home. I don't have to be *out* on errands to be busy. I can also be *in* on errands.

Slowly but surely I have grown to answer the phone less and less. When our bedtime routines have started, I no longer answer the phone. I just keep reading to my daughter.

When we sit down to a meal, I just let it ring and pass the potatoes. If I'm enjoying the company of a visitor, I'll often just ignore the ringing interruption and have another sip of tea. Later, when a good moment presents itself, I go and check on the messages. I've learned that if people have a vital message, I can trust that they will leave it for me. So far there has been nothing I've regretted having accessed belatedly. Almost everything truly can wait. And the trade-off, at least for us, was a more relaxed family, calmer work environment, and smoother school day.

Be good to yourself. Wanting to be accessible to family and friends doesn't mean you have to permit yourself to be a puppet, pulled in many different directions by strings in the hands of others. Take hold of those strings. Become your own gatekeeper. The payoff will be more calm and control in your day. And then, when you do make yourself available to others, you won't be giving them a frazzled, rattled response to their query. You'll be giving them a more valuable piece of yourself. You'll have had time to think through your response, to gather your thoughts, to check on availability, to seek out additional resources, or to pray. When you allow yourself the freedom to regulate your interruptions, not only do you benefit but so does everyone you touch.

Chapter 4

Awareness Statement #4:

We Need a School That Runs Itself

WARNING! WARNING! WARNING!

Not only am I a gloriously unregimented mom, I am also a gloriously unregimented mom who homeschools her children. As such, much of learning to love my gloriously unregimented self has involved discovering ways to streamline the administrative and educational processes of running a homeschool. I have been relieved to discover over the years that it is not impossible to be both highly distractible AND a homeschooling parent. If you, too, homeschool your children, the following two chapters provide ideas and suggestions that will multiply the already numerous joys of homeschooling. If you are not a homeschooler, however, you may find that the reading of these chapters may cause fatigue, frustration, and the utterance of such phrases as "Why am I reading this when I could be enjoying a spinal tap instead?" I urge you to go ahead and read them anyway. If your child is in public or private school, you may think that some of the homeschooling-related strategies that appear in this book may not apply to you. But the truth is that anyone who has children homeschools. You just do it after school and call it "helping with homework." You take your child to a science museum for enrichment. You get a video on improving study skills. In fact, we're all in the business of guiding and caring for our children and their education. Chances are, you won't have to look too far for the applicability for your unique situation. In truth, you could find many of the ideas in this chapter useful in any number of situations—concepts such as

- The value of a to-do list for the highly distractible child.
- Why your children *need* to do chores.
- How you can alleviate your need to inspect some of your children's chores and still have them completed well.
- How to use allowances to change behaviors.
- How peer pressure can become your friend.

But accept my warning that MUCH of the next two chapters is geared specifically for running a homeschool. If you are not a homeschooler, you might enjoy leaping straight to chapter 6. But if you are a homeschooler, leap with me instead into a homeschool that practically runs itself.

A friend of mine is a middle-school teacher in our local public schools. She had a problem with one of her students and wanted to develop a strategy with the mother to get this girl back on track. The teacher's sincere desire was that this child would be able to achieve her very best in life. The teacher tried several times with no success to call the mom at home. She reluctantly called the mother at work, was able to connect with her, and began to express her concerns about this child. When the teacher suggested that both the teacher and the mother needed to keep closer tabs on this child's successes and struggles, the mother made a statement I shall never forget. She defensively replied, "You act like I'm supposed to be a mother twenty-four hours a day!"

We may have a schooling period in our day. We may not. But we ALL seize teaching moments as they occur. And of course, such moments occur ALL DAY LONG, right up until our children drift off to sleep.

When my friend told me this, I responded, I'm sure, with a look of stunned incredulity. That one-sentence response could easily be the title of another book that would be the premise of a study providing insight and perhaps understanding of many of today's cultural problems. But what struck me as humorous is that in response to this mother's "I can't do this twenty-four hours a day," most mothers would have responded with a very sincere "You mean there's an alternative?" We may have a schooling period in our day. We may not. But we ALL seize teaching moments as they occur. And of course, such moments occur ALL DAY LONG, right up until our children drift off to sleep.

We can feel that schooling is our whole life. And in some respects that's a good thing. But for the gloriously unregimented mom, the more mundane details of schooling can gobble up our lives to such an extent that we never even get to enjoy the good stuff in homeschooling. Which brings us to the fourth Awareness Statement, which is that we need, as much as possible, a school that will run itself. Don't get me wrong here. My goal is not to be as absent as possible from my children and their schooling. What I really mean is that if we can get the maintenance items of schooling to take care of themselves, if we can get the kids to do more for themselves, if we can get the mundane and repetitive details to almost process themselves, we are freed up to be proactively involved in the fun stuff of school—the teaching, the activities, the projects, the creative, and the delightful. *That* is what I would rather spend my time doing.

To get the most from this chapter, keep in mind that what follows is simply *one* model for running a homeschool. There are as many approaches to homeschooling as there are homeschoolers. You'll probably find it best to pick and choose snippets from the model used here rather than seek to use it as a whole. So please peruse and choose what you'll use.

The Four Walls of Our School

The school that runs itself is built on four very basic and pretty obvious components. Four walls hold up this school.

> *Wall 1:* Have clear, daily "To Do" lists.
> *Wall 2:* Have a clear school time.
> *Wall 3:* Have a few simple rules and consequences visible to all.
> *Wall 4:* Have an exit check.

Let's go over each of these items and explain the whys and hows.

Wall #1—Have Clear, Daily "To Do" Lists

I have a highly distractible son. If I listed for you the top ten most useful things I ever did to better manage him and his schooling, on that list somewhere would certainly be to put up a list for him of "Things to Be Done Today." This turned out to be helpful in more ways than I could have at first imagined. Not only did it force me to be more organized about just what we were going to do that day, it gave him a much-needed ending. Without the list it just seemed to him that no matter how hard he worked or how well he focused, when he finally completed a task, it would appear to him that I just pulled another out of a hat. The work seemed endless to him. A clearly posted list gave him hope—light at the end of the tunnel—that the schooling day would indeed end at some point.

The other benefit to this system is that I would have my children check off the items as they completed them. I could then, with just a glance at the board, determine where they were in their completion of the day's activities. I didn't have to interrupt them to ask.

Wall #2—Have a Clear School Time

While this wall states that you need a clear school time, I am NOT saying that you need specific hours, such as 9 A.M.–2 P.M. You can do that, but that isn't really what I'm talking about. The important thing is that when Mom says school is in session, *only school things can happen.* Whenever school is in session, my kids know that they may not leave the schooling room unless either they are done or I've declared that school is no longer in session. Those are the only two choices.

When we first started the stay-in-the-room rule, my kids would often just forget. So we stuck a piece of red crepe paper across the door of the room we school in. It served as a gentle, visible reminder to stop at the door and think.

You might have a certain light you turn on that signals that school is in session. You might choose to have a regular schedule. You might ring a bell. But whatever you choose, it is helpful to your kids if they have an added *visual* reminder that while there's a time for fun, this is the time to get down to the business of schooling.

Wall #3—Have Simple Rules and Consequences Displayed

The third wall in a self-run schoolroom is a clear, visible, and simple set of rules. Make rules that work for you and your family's needs. Don't just adopt mine. But as a reference point, here are ours:

Rule #1:   We respect people. (That includes how we speak to, touch, treat, encourage, and interact with one another.)

Rule #2:   We respect property. (We don't carve our desks or draw on the walls, etc.)

Rule #3:   When school is in session, we do schoolwork only. (Building a bridge out of paper clips or playing a computer game won't cut it as schoolwork—unless of course, that was assigned.)

Rule #4:   We do not leave the schoolroom without direct permission. (In the past my kids would leave for valid or semivalid reasons, often never to return. This rule ended that.)

These rules are posted on the wall, and we refer to them for any behavior problem. Most important is that consequences are posted right up there with the rules. If a child breaks a rule, his first offense results in having to do one thing as punishment. If there is a second offense, it kicks up to another thing. I allow four offenses. After four I will assume that this child is not simply being forgetful but is actively seeking trouble. From here the child is dismissed from school for the day, is sent to his or her room, and suffers the unpleasant consequences, sometimes by way of the principal.

You might be thinking that being dismissed for the day would absolutely delight your children. They wouldn't have to do their schoolwork. They'd be thrilled. Perhaps. You might need to choose a different meaning for the concept of being dismissed. I've found that my children really don't like being left out of the action, even if that action is schoolwork. It might sound like fun to them for a few hours, but it does grow old. Furthermore, my children know that they will now fall behind in their scheduled work. If they are not up to date on

> **I feared that the rules might create an atmosphere of oppression.**

their work, they may not participate in our homeschool group activities, Boy Scouts, AWANA, and so on. For my kids, *that* is a real punishment. Use your God-given parental discernment as to just what would motivate your child.

I was concerned when I first began using this system that it would feel almost like I was running a little Soviet gulag here. I feared that the rules might create an atmosphere of oppression. I've since come to believe, however, that this feeling is the result of yet another of the insidious leftover influences from the 1960s: "Let little Reginald express himself freely on your white walls with his green crayon and hinder him not." I came to this conclusion because I eventually found that when I stayed focused on tight adherence to the rules, it *freed* us to enjoy schooling. The day wasn't punctuated by arguments. We didn't get off track such that we lost control of the day. And the kids stayed on task much better, which in turn allowed them to finish their work in far less time. Who wouldn't like that?

Wall #4—Have an Exit Check

Speaking of finished work, we now come to the fourth wall of our self-running school. The system will be totally useless unless you implement this last step, having an exit check. Your children must come to you, show you that they have checked off every item on their list, and upon request present any materials that you want to see for verification. This is the glue that holds the system together. Be fussy here. Make this accountability real. If something needs to be redone, have them do it. Eventually they'll get the idea that if they want some free time, they will have to do the work and do it well.

Smoothing out Everyday Tasks

Here are several other ideas that can help your family smooth out the everyday details of keeping your home together. (For you non-homeschooling moms that are still with me here—I've written these ideas with the homeschooling family in mind, but you'll find that you can easily adapt them to meet your family's needs.)

Make Chores Part of the Daily School List

The first and obvious statement made here is that your children need chores. This is not an issue of having them "help you out." Get rid of that mindset immediately. Learning how to clean a sink and sort laundry and change a vacuum bag is as worthwhile as learning how to add decimals. It is a vital part of a person's education. Don't handicap your children with the mistaken belief that doing chores is somehow an extra. If your children go off to college and find themselves incompetent in the skills of housekeeping, you've done them no favors.

Making chores part of the daily school list serves several purposes. First, children will never have a long list of chores for any one day. A bit of work each day, particularly when it becomes routine, hardly seems like work at all. Second, making chores part of the school list provides accountability. The children's chores will get done because your children know that their time isn't their own until they are done. If the children need to leave the school area to accomplish these chores, remember that they need your express permission to do so. And remember to use timers so that you and each child check with each other when ample time has passed for the chores to have been completed.

Allow Cross-inspections

This means that one child must okay the work of another and vice versa. My son and daughter share a bathroom, each complaining of the mess on the other's side. Now they are both responsible for inspecting and okaying the other's work. If they take the cross-inspection seriously, it settles the issues and the room looks great. If they use this as an opportunity to abuse their power, the inspections are never "okayed" and neither can end his or her school day. It ties them both up endlessly. The incentive is very high to work together.

Combine School Activities Whenever Possible

There are many opportunities here to meld individual activities into one action, reducing the overall workload. Sometimes we review the school lessons for all my children at once simply by playing Mother May I. The only way for children to advance is to answer the review question I've posed to them. Each child's questions come from the child's review material. Any game can be used this way, even board games. Your children roll the dice, but before they can advance, they must answer your review question.

I once heard of a mom using a great idea to review math for three different levels at once. The youngest child was quizzed on basic addition by adding two numbers shown to her on a flash card, let's say $3 + 5$. The second child has to provide the product of multiplying these same numbers. The oldest child, sitting and listening but not seeing the numbers, has to discern what two numbers when added together would make 8 but when multiplied make 15. Thinking backwards from the sum and product promotes great logic development as well as an ability to manipulate numbers easily in their head.

Don't forget the obvious. Have the children grade each other's work. When appropriate, have them teach each other. What a gift for them to realize that they have knowledge that is of value to another. What an opportunity to share. You may hesitate here, feeling that there is already enough sibling-based tension between these kids. But don't dismiss this too quickly. It may take a while, but again, if their free time is contingent upon successful completion of their assigned school tasks (in this case, the learning of a concept by their sibling), they will soon discover the value in a sincere effort at teaching. Otherwise, their school day will never end, and they will have no time of their own.

Have an In-Box

Make sure to have a specific container for completed work needing to be checked—not an In-Area on your desk. My biggest problem in the "Just-throw-it-on-my-desk" days was that I would pick up a piece of paper to file away and in doing so would often grab a second, unrelated paper at the same time (often my children's lovingly and painfully produced schoolwork). The second paper would then join the intended paper in a file, sinking into oblivion, only to be retrieved years later when I'd be culling and dumping files. Having a box for the express purpose of holding papers in need of checking can prevent such problems.

Use Allowances to Encourage Growth in Weak Areas

I know that opinions regarding allowances are quite varied and that this topic can really be controversial. There are some who believe that allowances should never be tied to housework or schoolwork, and that chores and schoolwork should be done out of a sense of family and duty. I appreciate and understand that perspective. There are others who say that in the real world you get compensated for levels of production. Being paid an allowance for work is no different. I appreciate that perspective as well. I frankly think either position can be used beneficially and without harm.

In our house we don't have an automatic allowance for our kids. We have used allowances—in other words, financial incentives—in connection with areas we wanted strengthened, sometimes school related and sometimes in other areas. Here are three examples:

1. My son needed improvement in writing. I had him produce a monthly newsletter and send it to friends and family. I was the editor and assigned some articles and research. My son was paid only when the issues hit the mailbox. He kept this up for two years and really strengthened his writing ability and research skills.
2. In the past my daughter was often shy with people. We tied her allowance to what we called "courage exercises"—asking the librarian a question by herself, placing an order by herself at a restaurant, saying hello to someone new at church.

3. Most recently I wanted more and better interactions between my two oldest children and their three-year-old sister. I developed a list of preschool activities that they could do together. If they do six or more from the list, the older two are compensated for having provided Emma with great developmental activities—just like in a preschool. Emma thinks she's suddenly become popular with her brother and sister, I get more time to do some of the things I need to do, and the older two have a revenue-generating activity that truly contributes to the family. Everyone is winning in this scenario.

Borrow Peer Pressure

Peer pressure has been given such a negative image, and justly so. Most of the time this pressure from peers results in bringing out behaviors we'd just as soon skip. Pressure to smoke, pressure to swear, and pressure to dress in certain ways are just a few of the many results from influence of fellow classmates. But in homeschooling I've discovered I actually missed some of the ways that peers can influence my children's behavior. In my mind I see

I like this kind of peer pressure.

my son sitting next to two best buddies. They've all been given an assignment and have been informed that they will not go out to recess until the work is done. This same assignment done at home with no buddies and without the threat of no recess to motivate him would take him two to three hours. But with the pressure of his peers' desire that he join them in play, the task is completed in twenty minutes. I like *this* kind of peer pressure. How about the pressure that results when you know you will have to read your report on King Tut to the entire class next week? That pressure encourages you to put forth your best effort so as not to look bad in front of your classmates. I like *that* kind of peer pressure. So how do we borrow the good pressures from the classroom without taking in all the bad? Here are four possibilities:

1. Share a school day with another homeschooling child. I found a mom who has a highly distractible child just like my own, and we share one school day each week. One week it's at her house and another week it's at mine. Our boys arrive at the other's house with an armload of books and assignments. Play breaks are scheduled throughout the day but are completely contingent upon a section of assigned work being done completely and done well. These days consistently result in all work being done quickly.

2. Create a Presentation Day within your homeschool support group. Consider a monthly meeting for your group at which each child must present something he or she has been working on. Not only does this motivate children to do well on whatever they've been assigned for this event, it gives them an opportunity to develop public speaking and presentation skills. A plus no matter how you look at it.

3. Create a simpler at-home "Presentation Night." In our family each child showcases information from several studied topics. Sometimes they solve new math problems on a white board. Sometimes they present their newly learned German vocabulary with the help of props. Other times they do a full twenty-minute, in-character presentation of someone from Civil War days. The key here is to make it a big deal. The whole family comes to watch. You record it on the video camera. Next week you review it in class to get ideas for an improved performance next month. And above all, you have fun.

4. Share a subject. Writing is especially difficult for one of my children. We've finally gotten to the point that he no longer loathes it and indeed has developed some skills that should eventually serve him well. But to this day, getting regular writing out of him is a challenge. Turns out, many other homeschooling moms have had this experience. That is why our local support group has organized a writers' workshop. We selected a video-based writing program and shared the cost between the families who chose to participate. We meet once a week to view the next lesson and receive the next week's assignments. But also, each meeting provides an opportunity for our kids to share what they've written in the previous week. There are a lot of writing materials and programs out there, and while it's certainly important to carefully consider what materials to use, I think that almost any writing program, because of the added element of weekly peer review, would result in great improvement for my kids.

These are just some of the ways you can create a school that keeps your children on task. Anything you can do to alleviate all the "let's get back on track" moments will allow you more time for "the good stuff": acting out today's history lesson as a play, baking cookies for a fractions discussion, drawing a giant-sized map of Italy on the driveway. As we'll look at more closely in the next chapter, having defined boundaries to your school day doesn't mean that you have to make the actual lessons structured, dull, and repetitive. It simply provides the railing along the race course so that the path of learning doesn't shoot off the track, out into the stands, and off into the woods. The thrill of learning "around the track" can and should be delightful and exhilarating.

Chapter 5

Awareness Statement #5:

Our School Stuff Must Be Organized Because We're Not

You may think after reading the previous chapter that our schooling day is fairly rigid, ordered, and regimented. But the truth is that I have a rigid infrastructure so that we can be more flexible in our actual schooling endeavors. All that the four walls of our school really address is exactly how we will conduct our schooling. They in no way address just what our schooling is going to be.

This chapter will help you determine what it is you're going to study. It will also cover a method of organizing all your various lists and planning materials. WARNING: If you are an unschooler, skip this chapter entirely! It will simply serve only to annoy. If you use a packaged curriculum, skip to the section entitled "Organizing All Your School Stuff." However, if you fall into any of the following categories, you may proceed.

If you

- are a more traditional schooler but use some of your own materials,
- worry about gaps in your child's education,
- want to be more certain of what your child has learned,
- want your child to generally follow the program used by another school because you intend to return him or her to the school at some point,
- want to be able to fly off onto a subject of interest but can never find your related materials, or
- love the eclectic approach and tend to jump here and there to follow the interest of your children,

then there should be something in this organizational plan that you can use.

Organizing Paperwork

Organizing paperwork (serious yawn) can be a little tedious. Why even bother writing about it? Because once the paperwork is organized, you are free to follow any interest that pops up in your schooling. Your stuff is organized. You can find what you need, and the momentum of the learning moment needn't be lost.

If you are a gloriously unregimented mom, it is possible...you may perhaps...at least once or twice...have found that staying on a long-term plan is not easy for you.

This has many approaches, and herein you will simply find one of them—the one we use. You can save yourself the steps found here by simply buying one of the many three-ring binders, complete with printed dividers, that are available from many homeschool materials providers. Or you can set up your own system, using information provided here as a starting point.

Some folks really need and even want a program that is completely laid out for the entire school year. They want the objectives and daily activities planned far in advance. There is nothing wrong, and indeed several things right, about schooling in this manner. But...if you are a gloriously unregimented mom, it is possible...you may perhaps...at least once or twice...have found that staying on a long-term plan is not easy for you. You have been known to step off your beautifully developed lesson plans to pursue a worthy topic, the study of which was piqued by the briefest of mentions in some other arena. "Why does ice float instead of sink?" "Why is the one-chambered heart of a lobster less efficient than the human's four-chambered version?" Great questions!

Which lead to the discovery of several books, websites, and cool experiments that begin to answer the questions. Who cares if doing all these neat things put us four weeks behind schedule. Look at what we've learned!

A great deal of just that kind of diversion occurs in our schooling. It could easily be dubbed the "Hop-Around Method." To be honest, I love it. When a topic grabs us, we run with it until we exhaust it (or it exhausts us). However, there is a downside in that this "delight-driven method" can leave…the…dreaded…gaps (the third biggest fear of new homeschoolers, preceded only by the second—poor socialization—and the first—will my bookshelves withstand the added weight of all this stuff?). I have learned to plug the gaps, but to do so requires knowing just what the fabric should look like when whole. Let's start at the beginning. What do we want our children to learn?

> **I have learned to plug the gaps, but to do so requires knowing just what the fabric should look like when whole.**

Those of you who know teacher-ese from your previous language studies will immediately recognize that word *objectives* as a pillar of the educational process. It shows up on just about every lesson plan ever made. Having clear objectives simply means you know *what* your child should learn as a result of the lesson. Then, of course, if you know what you want your child to learn, you also want to know in what order he or she should learn it. If you are working with a packaged curriculum, the publishers have probably already worked this out for you *and* provided a clear schedule to boot. But if you're like me, you have a real hodgepodge of materials. Your math and language may be a standard workbook, but for your science you might want to do a study of the human body early in the school year, maybe do one on insects a bit later, and then finish out the year with a cool study on volcanoes. You might plan to study a particular culture in depth, and finally you want your children to improve on their sketching and typing skills.

Certainly you need a plan. You may be thinking that I'm going to recommend that we gloriously unregimented moms become hyper-organized when it comes to our schooling plans to compensate for our own distractibility. Some may choose that path. I think it's a perfectly reasonable response to the downside of being a free-roaming thinker. But I suspect I'm going to surprise you here. Instead of compensating for my constantly changing plans with a massive plan of organization, I allow for many meandering path changes. In fact, I actually like them. There certainly are some moms who have their entire year laid out. Others work maybe three months ahead. I must confess to you in all honesty, for better or worse, that my materials (except for math) are laid out—are you ready for this—usually about a week or two in advance. I do have clear objectives for the end of each year, but how I will get from here to there is planned in detail only about a week ahead, with maybe a general idea of the next four weeks in my mind.

This isn't a mistake or even poor planning. Here's my reasoning. I like to be able to change direction if we stumble upon a sudden interest in something. I like to be able to stretch out a study that excites us more than I had anticipated. I like to have the time to relearn or review or cover from another angle any item that a child seems to be struggling with. I used to lay out my plan much further in advance, but with each passing week I made so many red slashes, scribbles, whiteout marks, and arrows pushing things into next week that my written plan became a useless document. So I gave in to the truth about myself—that I like a lot of flexibility. With each passing year I've become more of a "hopper" rather than less. In truth, I probably use this method too much for the comfort levels of most. But I have learned that virtually all homeschoolers like to hop to some degree. There are some really spectacular learning moments that occur when hopping.

If you plan far in advance and that works for you, stick with it. It has its benefits. But if you're like me and you don't have a complete forty-week plan written out, don't beat yourself up. The short-term-plan approach has some real advantages. And if you have a method that allows you to see what the finished product should look like when complete—in other words, if you know what you want your child to learn by the end of the year—filling in any gaps that appear in your hop-around method isn't difficult.

Choosing Clear Objectives for Your Children

Start by choosing clear objectives. How do you choose those objectives that measure your child's development in an area of study? What makes a good objective? What makes a bad one?

I sit down each summer with a stack of blank paper. At the top of each page, I write the name of one of the subjects that we intend to study. Then I begin to list the objectives, the precise goals, for each child in that subject for the upcoming year. In our study of language for instance, I don't want a goal like "Johnny will get better at grammar." Such an objective is almost useless. At the end of the year, how will I know whether Johnny is better? Or more specifically, how will I *measure* that Johnny is indeed better? I want something measurable. A better goal would read, "Johnny will be able to name the eight parts of speech and categorize one hundred words of my choosing into each of those eight parts." *That* I can measure. I will know whether we're successful in achieving this clearly articulated and specific goal.

What's a Scope and Sequence?

You might be thinking "How do I know what my child needs to learn next?" This is where a scope and sequence document comes in. Obviously you will need a road map of just where you want to end up by the completion of the school year. If you have a packaged curriculum, this is less of an issue for you because the publishers of that curriculum have already figured out the scope and sequence. If you're not familiar with those terms, let me explain them.

Every educational publisher, every public school, every private school, puts out some sort of scope and sequence. The scope is what things a child should learn in each subject. The sequence is the order in which he or she should learn them. They are *never* carved in stone. Don't ever let them put you in a panic. Some schools will hit ancient Egypt in the ninth grade, while others do it in the sixth grade. Many things are interchangeable, so don't feel you must be married to any one scope and sequence. (Math in particular, however, does need to build upon previous information, and generally those scope and sequence documents that you find regarding math will be similar.)

If you don't have a scope and sequence, you can get one. You can get several. You can get hundreds. Just go online, type in "SCOPE AND SEQUENCE," and you'll have more options than frankly you've ever wanted. At the vendor hall of most homeschool conferences, the providers of complete curriculum packages will most likely have one to hand to you. I have quite a collection of them that I have obtained from numerous sources, including vendors, newspapers, publishers, public school mailings, magazines, and community flyers. I like having several versions to use as a reference point. I use them to get a sense

> **If my children express a sudden interest in the life of Beethoven or the blight that caused the Irish potato famine, I need to be able to pull together my materials quickly, before the interest has passed.**

of direction in building the map of where *I* want my children to be by the end of the year. (And sometimes, I use them as packing materials in a shipping box!) I am not chained to any one scope and sequence, nor do I have my own scope and sequence planned out for all twelve years. I spend time each summer determining which subjects we will hit, how hard we'll hit them, and most specifically, exactly what I want my children to be able to do and to know by the end of the year.

Organizing All Your School Stuff

We need a great deal of material to plan, develop, record, and execute our objectives. We need a system that not only organizes our material but also allows us to retrieve it instantly at the moment it is needed. My material must be organized so that I don't have to be. If my children express a sudden interest in the life of Beethoven or the blight that caused the Irish potato famine, I need to be able to pull together my materials quickly, before the interest has passed. And I don't have the luxury of vast amounts of time needed to re-sort all our stuff every time a new topic is considered. So we need a system in which, just as my grandmother used to say, *everything has a place and everything is in its place.* (She also used to take her teeth out in public restaurants, so it's worth exercising caution in following her advice. But I think she's on target at least with the former.)

Nonetheless, I have a grandma-praiseworthy system that I really like in which everything I need to plan our school year is in one LARGE three-ring binder. No kidding. All in one place.

My binder has two basic sections:

1. *Subject-by-subject* section, which not surprisingly breaks up our entire schooling effort by subject (math, science, etc.)
2. *Master Resources* section, which has lists of absolutely ALL the resources I have gathered over the years, broken up into general and easily retrievable categories. (This is explained in detail later in this chapter.)

The subject-by-subject section is full of tabs, one for each subject ever studied, currently being studied, or intended to be studied in the next year or so. Here is how our tabs currently read after nine years of homeschooling:

ART	LIFE SKILLS
BIBLE	LOGIC
CHARACTER	MATH
DEBATE	MUSIC
ENGINEERING	PHYS ED
GEOGRAPHY	READING
GERMAN	SCIENCE
GOVERNMENT	SIGN LANGUAGE
HEALTH	SPANISH
HISTORY	SPELLING
LANGUAGE	WRITING
LATIN	VOCABULARY

Let me emphasize that we DO NOT study all of these topics at one time, but they are topics we have studied or are studying or will study. If something is taught in our school, it gets a section in my binder.

The first page in each subject section contains, as you might guess, a list of objectives. What do I want each child to learn in this topic in this year? The next page creates a list of the specific resources I have available that would help me accomplish my stated objective. I pull information from my master resources section to create this list. For example, in the math section I will have a page listing the objectives for each child. For one child my objectives might include "Can identify equivalent fractions." On my next page I will list the resources I have that will support this learning objective. While I may have eighty-seven math-related board games in my closet, I want to list only those games that would promote learning on *this* topic. The Counting Bears board game and Fun with Algorithms Bingo would not make this list.

Every resource that I have in my home will be fair game for this list. This would include computer games, board games, manipulatives, books, tapes, videos, and sometimes even people who are a great contact. We know of a woman who was in Holland during Nazi occupation. We plan to interview her on an upcoming study of World War II. We are also very friendly with our car mechanic. Guess what we have planned for him?

Putting this section together may sound overwhelming. In fact it would be overwhelming if you felt the need to do it all in one day. Please, don't do that. Create the sections in your three-ring binder and then add to them over time. Your kids can help. Have them take an inventory of all your board game titles or your educational videos. Then you can plug these resources into the correct section by simply reading through the list.

Three more dividers are placed at the back of my binder, covering

> FIELD TRIP IDEAS
> SUMMER IDEAS
> UNIT STUDY IDEAS

These three sections hold ideas for future use so that, once again, our brains don't have to. Now, when you read in the local newspaper about a neat place to visit and tear out the ad or article, or when you pick up a brochure on a wonderful museum nearby, you have a place to put the material. When you think of a fun summer activity to give the kids this year, you can jot it down and have a place to put it. When you read an interesting historical piece that tells of how the milkweed plant was used in World War II to stuff life vests and explains that the plant also doubles as the monarch butterfly's egg-laying nursery, and you decide that a study of the various uses of the milkweed plant would make a *wonderful* unit study, you now have a place to put it. If you think of a neat Christmas gift that you and your kids could make, it gets listed under possible summer activities. You get the idea, I'm sure. Almost anything that passes through your hands or your head that would be a great addition to your schooling will no longer be certain to be lost because...you have a place to put it.

Almost anything that passes through your hands or your head that would be a great addition to your schooling will no longer be certain to be lost because...you have a place to put it.

Finally, at the very front of the binder is a special little tabbed section called "TO DO." Any school-related task that I need to do gets written in this section. It will include such things as

- Create a science quiz to cover video we watched together.
- Order next workbook for Katie's math.
- Gather materials for kids to make a pretend passport for Thursday's geography lesson.
- Set up a cassette/learning station somewhere in the house away from the TV.
- Find a beginning tennis class.

You'll use this binder in its entirety when preparing for your next year. But you'll also use it all year long. You might be working through a textbook with your child and discover that the child really doesn't get some concept. Maybe your child needs more work on something but you find your textbook is out of material. What do you do now? Flip open your binder and look at your list of resources. You don't have to scan your shelves looking for something that you can't recall whether you even have and hoping that you can recall what it is. And remember those dreaded gaps? Every so often you look at your objectives and check off those that have been achieved. Those that remain will give you ideas for what to do in the next couple of weeks or months. Sometimes a unit study will be an obvious solution to hitting several different topics at once. I often find that our unexpected diversions covered several of the objectives I had recorded but in a much more fun and interesting manner than originally envisioned.

Having your stuff structured will allow you the freedom and the joy of following the delight of the moment without the added fear that everything will fall apart.

You might have a system generally like this but with these different components laid out in different places. If that works for you, that's fine. Over time, however, I ended up putting all my various components into this one three-ring binder because I found it so useful to have everything all in one place. I could pick up my work and take it with me to wherever we might be headed, without the usual searching and pulling from six different areas.

Every *thing* is organized so you don't have to be. Once you start putting your three-ring binder together, all those random, seemingly unconnected pieces of paper begin to gravitate there, seeking their own place. Having a system that "knows" where everything is will be your solid infrastructure. Having your stuff structured will allow you the freedom and the joy of following the delight of the moment without the added fear that everything will fall apart. And that, in turn, will allow you to put your energies into the things that have a more profound and meaningful effect on yourself and your family.

Chapter 6

Awareness Statement #6:

We Need Wider Margins

I first came across the idea of "margin" years ago when I read the book *Margin* by Dr. Richard A. Swenson. It pretty much confirmed most of what I already felt was happening in our own lives. Everyone in American culture could benefit from increasing their margins but the highly distractible mom even more so. We, more than others, need transition time. We don't usually engage in one intensive activity and push it to the limit. We have hundreds of less intensive activities that fill every available space in our day and our brains. Before we even answer one child's question, three more kids have thrown their questions into the mix. We don't have time to stop and redirect ourselves thoughtfully. The oatmeal is boiling over, the UPS man is at the door awaiting a signature, and the baby has just gone into the backyard without a diaper on. I would LOVE to be able to stop in between each task, turn my attention fully and thoughtfully to the next item needing my input, and give it my very best. That's what I got to do when I was working in the public arena. But life at home doesn't come in a distinct, segmented, and orderly fashion. The transition time that is available in most other arenas is not available to us. It's not available to any mom. But some moms can leave an activity for a moment, confront an issue that has suddenly appeared and then pop right back to the original activity. In other words, these moms have a back burner. But we gloriously unregimented moms, for whatever reasons, possess stoves that no longer come equipped with back burners—our stoves have only one burner. It's a front burner, and it's always on. For this reason we have an even greater need for margins.

> **We tend to live every hour of every day so packed from start to finish that there is no margin for error or change or spontaneity.**

What's a Margin?

Margin means the space that exists between our resources and our commitment of those resources. If you have seven days a week and you've committed something to fill six of those days, you have a one-day margin. If you make twenty thousand dollars a year and your commitments require eighteen thousand dollars of it, you have a margin of two thousand dollars. If your body needs eight hours of rest each night and you typically give it seven, you have a deficit margin.

We tend to live every hour of every day so packed from start to finish that there is no margin for error or change or spontaneity. Everyone is pushing the envelope to the edge—and suffering from a lack of margin. Futurist David Zach calls it "hyperliving," constantly "skimming along the surface of life."[1]

In his book Dr. Swenson quotes a cardiologist who prescribes for his Type A personality patients that

- they get in the longest line at the bank.
- they commit to listening to two people each day without ever interrupting them.
- they stop booking appointments back-to-back but leave a margin of time between each appointment.

My husband is a pretty classic Type A personality. He had a heart scare several years ago, and one of the best pieces of advice his cardiologist gave him was to throw away his alarm clock. If he needed to be getting up at a certain time, he needed to go to bed early enough so that he would naturally wake up by then. If you're on an irregular schedule dictated by others, that might be hard to accommodate, but it was some of the best advice my husband ever got. He had built up a pretty long-term sleep deficit that he needed to address, which this tactic eventually accomplished.

Since reading Dr. Swenson's book years ago, I made some changes in our family's way of doing things that gave us some of the margin that we now enjoy and that frankly I think we were starving for. The first really useful thing is to simply start thinking about margin and recognizing the lack of it in your life. Here are some simple ideas that can start putting the margin back into your life.

Putting Margin Back into Our Lives

Shoot for Early

Forget shooting for on time. Shoot for early. One of the benefits of homeschooling that I recognized early on was that we didn't have that morning let's-get-out-the-door frenzy that we had experienced getting my son ready for his traditional kindergarten.

Do you have your coat? How about your gloves? Good. Scarf? No? Run and get it. How should I know where it is? Try the floor of the hall closet. And don't forget your lunch. Okay, let's go. No wait… how could you not have brushed your hair? Find a brush (before my tethering days). Hurry, hurry, hurry, I see the bus coming. What do you mean you haven't had breakfast?!

> **But also of great value that should not be easily dismissed is the quiet pleasure of finding ourselves simply sitting in the car, waiting for others to arrive.**

What a joy to no longer have that as part of our existence. That was the first obvious and palpable benefit that I noticed when we began homeschooling. And I noticed it the very first week.

Then…Sunday came. Time for church…and there I was…doing it all again.

Now, if I know that we generally need fifteen minutes to grab everything and get out the door, I set a timer for twice that amount of time. It is my hope that we can avoid the frenzy, yes, but also I want to aim at arriving early for two good reasons. First, it allows margin for the unexpected. And if there's anything that you can expect in life, it's that the unexpected WILL happen:

- the diaper will leak unexpectedly.
- the yogurt will spill down the stairs.
- we will leave some vital item behind for which we must return home.

These things now don't throw a monkey wrench into my day.

Second, I have discovered a gift in arriving early. It might allow us to be of service to someone else in setting something up. But also of great value that should not be easily dismissed is the quiet pleasure of finding ourselves simply sitting in the car, waiting for others to arrive. Now that may sound odd in this hyper-efficiency, use-every-minute-to-the-fullest world. But when we find ourselves just sitting, the most wonderful thing happens—we chat. We tell knock-knock jokes. We roll down the window and try to identify the different birds that we hear. We applaud the baby who performed her ABCs song for us. Sad to say, today we label as "wasted time" what our great-grandparents used to call "fellowship" and "visiting." What a lost treasure.

Home Sweet Home

Caring parents want to be sure that their children have every opportunity to become their very best. However, this can translate into having way too many things on an educational to-do list. My list always gets a bit longer after I have read about one of those impressive families in homeschooling magazines. I come away thinking that it's not enough to just teach reading, writing, and arithmetic. I also have to have my

> **Where do we live? Do we live at home?**

kids create a 3-D model of the atomic structure of each element, disassemble and reassemble the family car, and feed a growing herd of long-haired alpacas.

There seems to be a pressure on all parents to be fearful of what our kids might be missing. As a result we often overextend them. We find ourselves exhaustedly piling them into the car for another round of deliveries to piano lessons, tennis lessons, art classes, voice, violin, karate, youth group, science day camp, vacation Bible school, soccer camp, etc. Home can become like the center of a wheel that you touch briefly as you fly off onto another spoke. The question can then become, Where do we live? Do we *live* at home? Or does life really occur at the edge of the wheel, and home is just a refueling zone where we grab something as we head back out to the edge?

When we moved this last time, we left a situation in which we had been overextended. We'd been quite involved in our church and even more heavily in our homeschool support group. My first book had just come out, we had a new baby, and we had also just moved. Needless to say, we were pretty fried. So we didn't hurry into getting involved in our new location. Instead we took some time to breathe. When you add to this the fact that we moved to New England in the dead of winter, meaning it was a major production just to get out of the driveway, we decided to just stay home. We really turned inward for a time. During this period I fell in love with being home with my family. The phone didn't ring. We didn't know anyone. We had no place to go. We hadn't yet developed a social life. So we just stayed home and played board games and built snow forts. We read to each other. We cooked together. Staying home made me aware of a treasure I hadn't even appreciated was there.

I know of a homeschooling family that made being home one of their top priorities. They had six children with many and varied talents to develop. They wanted to support the abilities of these children with private lessons for their various endeavors. But they also wanted to avoid the frenzy of constantly going here and there for different forms of instruction. So they made a simple rule. Tutors of their children had to be willing to come to their home. I really grew to respect this choice. It clearly required putting their money where their values were because sometimes they had to pay extra for this arrangement. It also meant that sometimes they couldn't get their first choice of teacher and had to find another. But in the end they felt the payoff was worth the compromises. While they certainly went out for shopping, errands, church, and family functions, they were still able to minimize the "life on the road" that so many of us are currently living. Their family and their home were the center of their lives, the grounding and anchor for all that life brings. I've tried to keep alive the pace and comfort that came from our quiet early days in New England. I've made a commitment to try to stay home at least three days a week. This simple act has often brought the needed time to unwind, to unencumber our minds, to touch base with each other as a family. It has also meant that we've had to say no to quite a few things.

Saying no takes some practice. When someone asks you to do something, even if you expect you'll eventually say "Yes," start by simply saying, "I need to check my schedule and my husband's. Let me give you a ring." Now you have time to decide whether it's really something you want to spend your time on. Is it worthwhile enough of a project to justify the time away from your family? A need is calling, but it may not be God's calling for you. So always start with a "Let me check." Make that your consistent, standard response. This habit might save you from letting a "Sure, I'll do it" slip out when a "Not this time" would have been better.

Jealously guard your time with your family. And don't feel the need to apologize for it. The phrase "You can't take it with you" warns about placing too much emphasis on the things of earth. That declaration misses one very important exception. While there's practically nothing you have here that you'll see in heaven, there is one thing—your children. Isn't that astounding? I won't see my meticulously prepared dinner. I won't see the smoothly running co-op schedule. I won't see my neat and tidy closet, no matter how much energy and effort I put into its organization. But with a hope and a prayer, I *may* actually see the faces of my children. Never apologize for putting your investments where they can make an eternal difference—in your family.

> **If anyone utters the words, "I'm bored," Boredom Day is instantly declared.**

Learn to Love Boredom

There is a jewel, a treasure that you may possibly have not yet discovered. Have you found the deeply buried secret that lies in boredom? Somehow this culture of parents has decided that a bored child is something to be dreaded. We feel this pressure to have our children perpetually entertained as a sign of our own excellent and creative parenting. And what's worse, the children come to believe that life is to be a constant stimulation with the same rapid changes they experience with television. I LOVE boredom in our house. I sometimes even declare a Boredom Day. This means that my kids cannot play on the computer, no friends may come over, and there is no TV. In fact, we have an unspoken rule in our house that if anyone utters the words, "I'm bored," Boredom Day is instantly declared. The kids might spend an hour or so whining, but sooner or later, once enough time has passed, they eventually allow the boredom to motivate them to creativity—to rather large bursts of creativity, I might add. Some of the most wonderful projects that my children have concocted and immersed themselves in have been borne on the wings of boredom. (My personal favorite was the chain reaction device that took over an entire bedroom, not to mention several hours of an otherwise entirely boring day!)

Learn to love boredom. Seek it out. If it doesn't happen on its own, create it. If you take it upon yourself to fill that vacuum called "boredom," your children won't learn the delight and gift that come from exercising their imaginations or the confidence that comes from knowing that they can entertain themselves.

Schedule Laughter

In our house, laughter seems to be around every corner. My family is funny without ever meaning to be. Not too long ago I went on a diet and found, miracle of miracles, that I had quickly lost fifteen pounds! I was giving my husband a hard time for not having taken notice. (To his great credit, he likewise makes no notice when I gain pounds.) But at his expense, I was playfully needling him, resulting in mock defensive statements from

The Proverbs 31 woman knew the value in laughter. Do you?

him. My son, fearing that I truly might have felt injured, rallied to my defense. "I could tell you'd lost weight, Mom. Maybe Dad couldn't, but I could tell. You look great. It's completely obvious you've lost weight. Your skin is so flabby now." The needling of my husband completely stopped. In stunned silence, I swung my head to look at my son. You could see the blood drain from his face. He knew he'd said something wrong but hadn't a clue what it was. Then I burst into laughter. With a family like this, mirth abounds.

Did you know that the Proverbs 31 woman laughed? It's seldom stressed in discourses on this passage. Instead, her many other qualities are held up before us as a role model of great worth (i.e., great guilt?). Usually what we hear is that she is eager to work, provides for her family, brings her husband respect, and clothes her children beautifully. Of course, the first thing to leap out to most of us moms is that she had servants! You'd be surprised at the extraordinary list of things I could get done if someone else was actually doing it for me. But almost never mentioned is the fact that this clearly hardworking woman laughed. Why did the scriptures include that? I think that if she gave so much of herself to her family but did it in anger or bitterness or guilt, then the whole picture of this role model would be incomplete. God loveth a *cheerful* giver. This woman's own soul was also fed. She laughed. She must have studied, because she spoke with wisdom and faithful instruction was always on her tongue. The Proverbs 31 woman knew the value in laughter. Do you?

A Loma Linda University study demonstrated that the act of laughing increased disease-fighting white blood cells by 25 percent. The past ten years have produced many studies supporting the value of laughter to longevity as well as the opposing increased rate of death for those who regularly experience anger and stress. Anger causes a squeezing of blood vessels. Conversely, laughter pumps the heart, exercises the muscles of the abdomen, chest, shoulders, and neck, increases circulation, and, perhaps best of all, releases pleasure-inducing endorphins and improves the immune system.[2] Whew! What a list. But there's no surprise in this is there? Proverbs 17:22 says, " [A] cheerful heart is good medicine." Proverbs 15:15 says, "[T]he cheerful heart has a continual feast."

> **When the strain and drain of too many weeks without laughter makes itself obvious, I now actually put laughter on the schedule. I consider it a biblical mandate.**

God made us with so many needs that bring us great pleasure when they are filled. We become tired. He provided the glorious refueling blessing of sleep. We become hungry. He provided a diversity of provision as to continually amaze our palate. We become low in spirit. He provided the undeniable and delightful release of laughter. Why, oh why, do we think we know more than God? Why do we believe that we can get by with less sleep and eat differently than He intended? And why do we go days, weeks, and months without laughing?

I have watched stress accumulate in my husband's life from time to time, depending on the various work-related projects in his schedule. At one point it became obvious to me that he *needed* to laugh. I came to believe it was actually vital. So I put it on the schedule. I taped some of the shows that make him laugh (I hesitate to tell you about the very juvenile Three Stooges type of material that fills him with laughter) and made him sit and watch and laugh. The shows did nothing for me, but seeing him laugh so hard that he fell over sideways onto the couch filled me to overflowing. It *was* good medicine. It did improve the quality of his life, which in turn improved the quality of all our lives.

When the strain and drain of too many weeks without laughter makes itself obvious, I now actually put laughter on the schedule. I consider it a biblical mandate. I schedule a family night, make or order some fun food, and pop the popcorn. We watch something that is sure to bring laughter to our throats. And every time I do it, I come away wondering what made me think I could put it off for so long.

Little Tips That Save Time

Time is probably one of the resources we push the hardest. Scores of books out there give us time-saving tips. There's the Hints from Heloise, and of course Martha Stewart, and there's even Mark Lowry. I hope you're familiar with Mark Lowry. He's a funny, funny Christian comedian who was with the Gaither Vocal Band for years, made many videos, and so on. Check him out at his own website, www.marklowry.com.

Mark Lowry likes to compare and contrast himself with Martha Stewart. One of Martha's suggestions praised the many uses of Alka Seltzer tablets. She says you can drop them in your toilet and in twenty minutes—swish and you're done. You can drop them in a vase or a thermos and clean that nasty stuff on its hard to reach bottom without ever reaching in your hand. You can even clean your jewelry. Mark, clearly an unashamed bachelor, says he just puts his jewelry, vases, and thermoses in the toilet, adds the Alka Seltzer, and takes care of the whole bunch at once.

I am hopeful that my suggestions will be slightly more appealing. They're just little changes, little tips, but if you make a lot of little changes a part of your habit, their cumulative effect can be substantial. Here are a few of my favorites:

Have a church bag. Assemble all that stuff that you often run back for or wish you'd brought along (in ours I keep diapers, wipes, Cheerios, two missionary books, character-building comics that I permit my kids to read if they're squirrely in church, a mini-medicine pack, and granola bars to eat en route if someone missed breakfast). It might be worth having an extra pair of socks and a hairbrush in there too! Ya think?

Streamline food preparation. There are many ways to streamline food preparation in your life. And if any of you have been able to execute one of those once-a-month-cooking programs, I must tell you that I think you practically walk on water. I am so impressed with people who can pull that off. And performing these well-planned cooking events do indeed free up a lot of time.

> **I still have the sixteen-pound can of tuna sitting on my pantry shelf approaching its expiration date.**

I just can't do it. I can't seem to get that organized. It requires thinking far, far ahead of my usual two-minute plan of action. You have to choose your family's favorite menu and multiply all the ingredients by a chosen number so that they will now make forty-two meals instead of just one. And then…and then.. there's the grocery shopping list you need to create. I'm sure that when this process has been done a few times it becomes easier. I have no doubt that women who do this are well rewarded by the simplicity of their meal-making efforts between these two- to three-day cooking marathons. As for me, I still have the sixteen-pound can of tuna sitting on my pantry shelf approaching its expiration date.

However, I did find a wonderful tip in Terri Camp's book *I'm Going to Be the Greatest Mom Ever!*[3] and it's so me—because it takes virtually no planning. Terri takes one day a month and cooks meat. That's it. That's the whole plan. She cooks twenty-four pounds of ground beef, four roasts, and six chickens. When they're cooked, she bags them in meal-sized quantities and freezes them. When it's time to make a meal, she can pull out a bag, and almost any recipe can be accomplished in less than twenty minutes. I don't plan this type of cooking day. I don't even think ahead. When I'm at the grocery store and realize that it has been a while, I load up on meats, and that day becomes my cooking day. Yes, it does take a whole day of being at home, but it doesn't eat up your whole day to accomplish. While things are simmering or cooling, I'm off doing other things.

Keep a cooler in the car. This allows me some latitude of time. If I have four or five places to go, I prefer to hit each of these stores in the most efficient route. With the cooler, I can follow the logical route. Otherwise, I would have to make the food store last on the route so I could minimize the time the food is unrefrigerated.

Clean the car while you wait. We often pile the whole family into the car and take a little outing, maybe to do errands, maybe for a run to get ice cream. But by the time we've arrived, the youngest one has fallen asleep for a much-needed nap. On a fairly regular basis I find myself sitting in the car with a napping toddler while one or more of my family members run inside to accomplish some shopping task. At one point I tried to keep a book in the car so I'd have something to do with my solitude. But when I'd get interested in the book, it would then follow me into the house and somehow never make it back to the car. More successful, however,

Think outside of tradition and make it work for you.

has been my stash of cleaning supplies. I now keep a stiff brush, a few rags, a bottle of vinyl cleaner, and a bottle of window cleaner in the car at all times. Whenever I find myself waiting in my car, I do a quick little cleaning of the interior. The windows finally get that layer of oily film wiped off. The brush is used to swiftly escort the many crumbs from my carpet down and onto the pavement. I don't have a regular car clean-out on my cleaning schedule (cleaning schedule???), but with this little backup system, I find that my car gets cleaned out about once a week or so.

Shop during off-hours. Shopping on the weekend takes at least twice as long as shopping during the week. Consider shifting your family's patterns to accommodate this fact. If you're a homeschooling family and are schooling Monday through Friday, chances are you do your shopping on Saturdays, the most crowded and frenzied day to shop, with the added blessing of standing in the longest lines of the week. You probably don't have to follow the traditional days of schooling. (If your state does require it, skip this one.) We made a plan a few years back to school on Saturday and take off Wednesday or Thursday instead. We get to hit the stores early in the morning on low-crowd days. The kids get a break mid-week, and we stay home on Saturdays, when the shopping crowds and even the traffic are worth avoiding. The freedoms of homeschooling are yours to manipulate. Think outside of tradition and make it work for you.

Keep liners under liners. Once, while sitting in a hospital waiting room, I watched as a janitor pulled a full trash bag from a can, reached right down inside the can and pulled up a fresh, new liner. What a smart idea! So now, when I need to place a new liner in a can, I put five or ten more at the bottom of the can first. This saves many steps later on.

Prevent bath time from wasting your time. I used to put my kids in the tub and then sit and sit and sit—or worse yet, rest on my now aching knees. One day, in desperation to complete some cooking task while bathing a child, I hit upon an idea that worked. Since my kids were now able to sit up quite safely, I started bathing them in a big Rubbermaid tub (about two feet by three feet) in the middle of the kitchen (but nowhere near where I handled hot foods). The first benefit was that the risk of their falling out was almost nil because the sides of the tub were so much closer and higher than those of the bathtub. In addition, my kids thought it was great fun because it was more like being in their own boat than in a bathtub. Furthermore, I never felt the need to rush them because I was still able to work and keep a watchful eye. It was no longer an either/or proposition. Lastly, when wiping up the bits of splashes, my floors got clean. My children loved it. My kitchen loved it. My knees loved it. Worked for me. Our great, great, great-grandparents would probably wonder why we took the tub out of the kitchen in the first place. It's an old idea that still works.

Save return address labels. When Christmas cards start rolling in this December, simply tear off the return address label from the envelope and tape it to the back of the card. Pitch the envelope. You only want to look at the cards anyway. Then, when you're ready to send something back to these folks, you don't have to find your address book. You don't have to stare at your address book's previous listing for this family and wonder whether they've moved...wonder whether your listing is current...wonder where you put that envelope. Skip all that and flip the card over.

Start a "Thinking About It" file. You get that favorite catalog in the mail. There's at least...what...maybe eight thousand things you're pretty sure you need. You fill out the order form and mail it off. It almost feels like you've launched a ship that will one day return to port, loaded with goodies and the stress of the bill. I am a bona fide book and curriculum junkie. Everyone has their obsession. I don't need furs. I don't care for jewelry. I shun cruises and exotic vacations. Don't bring me flowers. I am, by and large, a low-maintenance wife. But by gummy, I *love* school materials. And I've never met a book that I didn't like either. Many is the time I've cruised through the vendor hall of a state convention, picking up this and that and this and that, only to discover two years later that I used only this but not that or that. One of the most useful things I've ever done was to create a "Thinking About It" drawer. Any order I'm considering goes into this drawer. I simply allow some time to pass. Once the initial appeal has aged a bit, I'm better able to determine what is really going to be useful in our lives and what is mere fancy.

I use this drawer for almost any potential purchase: a new chair, curtains I'd like, a jacket I've considered ordering. Sometimes simply by the passing of time, I've stumbled upon the same or similar item at a greatly reduced price. Waiting is almost never regretted. And the payoff is a calmer and more reasoned approach to making your purchases.

Collect your favorite recipes. I have around forty cookbooks and a very extensive recipe card collection. Over the years certain recipes have proven themselves to be family favorites. There's worm soup (worm-shaped dough noodles...don't panic). There's that egg and hashbrown casserole that is a must for any brunch. And then there's the caramel popcorn that you can make in the microwave. You would think I would have known where these recipes were. Nonetheless, I often found myself slamming shut a third, a fourth, a fifth cookbook and mumbling, "Which book is it in?" I finally solved the problem when I took a three-ring binder and created the "Family Favorites" cookbook. I made copies of my family's favorite recipes and put them in pocket folders that are divided into typical cookbook groupings. When all is said and done, there are really only about thirty-five recipes that have become staples in our dining routines. And now I can find them in eight seconds flat.

> **Thankfully, once we recognize the need for margin, discovering a few strategies for finding it can be easy.**

For distractible moms, saving time and creating wider margins is not just a good idea, it's a necessity. If we don't take control of the flow of our day, we'll be forever chained to that sense of frenzy and muddle with which we often coexist. Once you've breathed in the calm of a completed, linear thought, you'll want it more and more. Thankfully, once we recognize the need for margin, discovering a few strategies for finding it can be easy. But sometimes there is more at stake than simply ridding ourselves of frenzy and muddle. Sometimes chaos overtakes the well-being of our homes and our families. If this is the case for you, you might want to consider making a few of the more significant changes that I suggest in the next chapter.

Endnotes

1. David Zach, as quoted by Richard A. Swenson, MD., in *Margin: Restoring Emotional, Physical, Financial, and Time Reserves to Overloaded Lives.* (Colorado Springs, CO: NavPress, 1992) page 146.

2. Michele Meyer, "Laughter—It's Good Medicine," *Better Homes and Gardens,* April 1997. Berk, L. (1989) "Neuroendocrine and Stress Hormone Changes During Mirthful Laughter," American Journal of Medical Sciences, 298(6), 390—396.

3. Terri Camp, *I'm Going to Be the Greatest Mom Ever!* (Oregon: Loyal Publishing, Inc., 2000), page 31.

Chapter 7

Awareness Statement #7:

We Might Need to Get Radical

My hope is that most of you are reading this book to pick up an idea here and there to integrate into your life. You might be a little frazzled, but you have no real crisis. I know, however, that is not the case for all of you. I've met some of you at conferences. I've sympathized with you as you've described the disorder of your home, your school, and your schedule. I've felt the anguish with you as you've expressed your very real concern that the chaos in your life is actually damaging relationships in your family. If you are at a point where you don't quite know how to regain control, one of the ideas in this chapter just might be what you need. While the suggestions here are clearly more radical, they also provide the greatest leap toward adding margin to your life.

Operation Neat-and-Clean House

If your issue is a disordered house, stop trying to fix it on your own. Take on the proven system of another. I must caution you, however, to proceed carefully. There are many great sources out there for ordering a home, but most are written by people who are naturally ordered in the first place. Indeed, it's very hard for them *not* to be organized, which means they don't have a clue what it's like to be me.

These naturally organized people have these extraordinary and impressive huge systems that they assure me are quite easy to live with once I go through the effort to put a system in place. The problem is that the systems were created for the naturally organized person. I've made my all-purpose, multitasking Cleaning Apron of Wonder, only to lose some of its required components after three uses. I've made the 3 x 5 filing system of chore organization that when covered with a comforter could double as a daybed. I would dutifully pull out my cards for the day and wilt at the prospect of completing all the chores written on them. The biggest problem in any of these radical, all-encompassing programs is that they assume I can stay on task for at least two hours at a shot. They have the wrong woman. Defeated once again, in the end I come away certain that somewhere I am depriving a village of a much-needed idiot.

> **Defeated once again, in the end I come away certain that somewhere I am depriving a village of a much-needed idiot.**

I cannot tell you that I like house cleaning. In fact, I'm more of a mind with Erma Bombeck, who said that with regards to house cleaning her second favorite task is ironing, her first being hitting her head on the top bunk till she faints. Nonetheless, I have finally found the system that works for a mind like mine (be kind). It's called the Fly Lady and can be found at www.flylady.net. It's free, it works, and it's funny. Once you join her program, she e-mails you every day with your assignments and encouragement. Her sense of humor comes ringing through, along with clear instructions for putting order in your home.

One of my favorite assignments is called the 27 Fling Boogie. You go through a specific room, carrying a garbage bag into which you put twenty-seven things to be either given away or thrown away. To free yourself from the chains that hold each item fast to your life, this boogie is best accomplished if you are singing "Please Release Me" at the top of your lungs while you toss. I now am on a first-name basis with the folks at the Goodwill store and the local Crisis Pregnancy Center. Both have been on the benefitting end of my boogie-ing.

The kernel of why the Fly Lady's system works is that it develops efficient cleaning habits tied to things I'm already doing. And most important, it starts small. There is no huge reorganization that must take place before you can even begin to apply her principles. You needn't even follow all her recommendations at once. In fact, she suggests that you don't. You start at the beginning and do what you can. I personally have utilized only one-fifteenth of the program, but I've done it religiously since I started, and it changed my house so radically that my husband is still commenting.

Boot the Box

You've heard over and over and over. TV eats huge chunks of our lives. I have to say that even I've grown weary of the ditch-TV diatribes that I've heard. I am an unashamed believer in using some videos and shows to enhance the learning in our schooling, particularly with history and science. But we cannot dismiss the amazing statistic that the average American adult would gain *thirty hours a week* if his or her TV were turned off. Even if you're a fan of selective television usage like I am, that is still a very unsettling number.

You want to do something radical and life altering? Unplug your TV for two months, with the understanding that it will come back on after that point if you still want it to. It will take a while to wean everybody from the various shows to which he or she has become addicted. It will take even longer to develop healthier alternatives to fill this now very open time. But it will happen. And you might never turn your TV back on.

Widen Your Financial Margin

Doesn't that sound lovely. You might think I'm suggesting you increase your income. That's one way. But then other margins in your life would surely suffer. I'm not suggesting you try to live under your means. No, this is much more radical than that. I'm suggesting you live WAY under your means. This is an unpopular concept. The American ideal is to expand to the width of your means and then work like crazy to increase your means once more, so that you can again expand to the width of your means.

When I reached the point where I decided to stop working and stay home, I knew I needed to address our spending because our income was going to take a hit. I linked up with a thrift-encouraging newsletter by Amy Dacyczyn called "The Tightwad Gazette," which was later turned into a very popular book.[1] I'd seen Amy on some

> I found that almost everything I wanted to do I could still do, only less expensively if I simply stopped and thought about it.

talk shows and watched audience members reel backwards in horror and disbelief at the lengths to which this woman would go to save money. But here's what got me. Pay attention to the numbers. In a seven-year period early in her marriage, her husband's annual income plus her own equaled less than thirty thousand dollars a year. During this seven-year period, the couple saved (take a deep breath) cash in the bank (take another deep breath) forty-nine thousand dollars. In just seven years! In addition they made several major purchases of vehicles, appliances, and furniture! When I learned what this woman had accomplished, I no longer cared what those audience members thought. THIS woman knew something that I wanted to know.

I dove into high-level thrift. I totally changed my grocery shopping habits. I made my own diaper wipes. I washed and reused my ziplock bags. We made our own gift-wrapping paper. We made our own gifts. We instituted Friday Pizza Night, and I actually got pretty good at homemade pizza. (My version costs between one and two dollars per large pizza, depending on the toppings. See the recipe at end of the book.) I found all the best thrift stores in the area. I found ways to buy books, take vacations, and eat out in new and less expensive ways. In fact, I found that almost everything I wanted to do I could still do, only less expensively if I simply stopped and thought about it.

In the end, the biggest thing I took away from learning to put thrift into my life was the wondrous gift of the absence of the stress that comes from living too close to one's financial margin—a relief I had never known before. It was like a giant exhale. I no longer panicked if the car unexpectedly needed repairs. I no longer felt chained to the Christmas gift and birthday party extravaganzas that I had witnessed in recent years. And even with our now greatly lessened income, the dollars in our bank account actually began to rise along with our emotional freedom. I felt free from the coveting that TV and magazines and the general material push of society had created in me. For the first time I felt I was practicing good stewardship. And if God moved me to give to someone or to some cause, I was able to.

> **Tell friends that you are going to become a temporary hermit and that they should not take your lack of communication personally.**

While some would look upon my choices as too much of a sacrifice, I believe the real sacrifice is in living life too close to the edge. I will now go to considerable lengths to never again feel that monthly bill-paying angst, to never again carry debt. Now that I've learned the peace that comes with that exhale, I never again want to hold my breath.

Drop Off the Face of the Earth

I will grant you that this is a particularly radical move, so radical that it shouldn't be entered into lightly. You might decide that a specific element of your life is so important that it deserves or even requires undivided attention. Maybe it's more time with your husband. Maybe it's decluttering your home. Maybe it's a time to declutter your life because your current pace and schedule have you headed on a crash course for disaster. If you need to turn something around in a big way, declare a sixty-day virtual vacation. Let everyone know that you will be disengaging for a time to regroup, reconsider, redefine, and relax. Tell friends that you are going to become a temporary hermit and that they should not take your lack of communication personally. Explain that you need some time to turn inward and recharge.

Turn your answering machine on (volume completely down) with a new message that says you are unavailable for a time for a much-needed vacation. Pull out of every engagement possible on your calendar. Postpone, change plans, or cancel. Don't open any mail that isn't a bill. You may find that during this time you will have to quit doing some things that you enjoy. However, the tradeoff at the end will possibly change you forever as you relink with your family, as home becomes the anchor in your life that it was intended to be rather than the touchstone we hit upon as we fly off to another place.

Force Yourself Into Accountability

Almost the opposite of the dropping-off-the-face-of-the-earth strategy is arranging for accountability in your life. I love this one because it caters to how we women are wired. I respond differently when other people are involved than if I were acting alone. I have found that if I involve other people in areas of my life where I really don't want to let things slide, I'm much more likely to stick to my own goals. Here are some ways I've used this powerful motivator.

> If I involve other people in areas of my life where I really don't want to let things slide, I'm much more likely to stick to my own goals.

Students: The More the Merrier

If your concern is that your homeschool is not running as smoothly as it should, consider *taking on another student.* That certainly sounds counterintuitive. If you're having problems handling the four kids in your school, how could having five make it better? Let me tell you how this worked for me. There were zero little girls in our neighborhood, and I grew tired of watching my daughter's sad little face as her brother went off to play with any number of little boys who lived around us. I asked a family at our church if they would consider allowing their little girl to join our school. They agreed, and soon I was homeschooling this little girl along with my own three days a week.

My initial objective was simply to provide a much needed playmate for my daughter. That was truly my only goal. Beyond the play value, I had no idea the impact this action would have on our homeschool. But what I soon discovered was that my organization, my teaching, and my results were many times greater. Why?? Because I was accountable to another adult. At the end of each day, when the other mom picked up her child, I felt compelled to give her a list of just what we had accomplished. Knowing that another adult would be privy to our actions that day, I made certain we'd had some worthwhile actions to report.

We will often let things slide within the privacy and cocoon of our own family that we would not otherwise let slide. If you know that you would be likely to produce a better educational product just because someone else is watching, this might be an excellent option to consider. The blessing is that often families are out there hoping for just such an arrangement. Many winners can result in a setup like this. Obviously, before you take this suggestion and apply it, you must be certain that the laws in your state permit it. Check first with HSLDA (Home School Legal Defense Association at www.hslda.org).

Polly Put the Kettle On, We'll All Have Tea!

Just as having another child in my home raises my standards, so does having company. In fact, I've stated in my workshops that this is pretty much the only time I dust. If you need a regular "check" in your home-keeping system, schedule company as often as you need it to keep yourself following your own system. Schedule some play dates at your home. Set up a weekly moms' tea. Invite over that new family who came to church last week. Whatever strikes your fancy.

Exercise Buddies

I'm not going to be noble here. I hate exercise. I really do. When I see others engaged in it, I am skeptical that I am witnessing an honest pursuit of health but rather believe I am observing an obsession with the trendy image du jour. At least that's what I tell myself when I become winded just climbing the stairs. Nonetheless, I *know* I really need more exercise. But does it have to be so dreadfully boring? Even if I strap a set of headphones over my ears and pipe in something of extraordinary interest to me, I can still find several good reasons why I just can't make it to the track (treadmill, aerobics video, Irish dance video, tai chi, tie dye, take your pick) today. I solved that problem, however, when I joined some of my friends. We all agreed to meet at 8 A.M. at the track. Pretty much, that was all it took. Somehow, just knowing that someone else will know when I've thrown in the towel again keeps me going back every morning at eight. Can you imagine how much more I would accomplish if I had to turn in a list of what I ate each day? No sense getting carried away.

There aren't many opportunities to improve your character and your waistline at the same time.

This particular group has developed in another useful way. We hold each other accountable for more than exercise. Since all three of us are Christians, we share prayer requests, we seek godly counsel on life's issues, and we take on assignments that will help us grow in our roles as mothers and wives. It is expected that we will report back on the accomplished task. If this isn't done, we have to answer to someone. This kind of accountability is a gift and a trust. It can be a mighty tool in developing your personal walk with the Lord. Be oh so careful to avoid the very real danger of calling this time together "sharing" when it really could become a time to gossip or a major venting session. Craft your conversation carefully with an unwavering commitment to godly behavior and an expectation of complete and total confidentiality. You don't *need* to tie this time to exercise, but what a great plus. There aren't many opportunities to improve your character and your waistline at the same time.

Internet Accountability

One of the best ways to use today's leap in technology is to create accountability via e-mail. Find a buddy who also wants the oh so slight pressure of accountability. Select a Bible study or a book to study. Agree upon a schedule for progressing through the material. Lastly, decide upon a meeting point. Will you be in contact daily? Weekly? Consider having several in your group. But don't get so many that you won't be missed if you step out. The accountability factor drops after a certain number. Use what works for you.

An Appointment with God

You've probably heard that you should have a regular, quiet time with God *soooooo* many times that it barely registers anymore. I understand that. Really I do. In my head I agree that this is important. If you ask me very directly, I will state unabashedly that this is a *very* important part of a Christian's walk. No doubt about it. Now ask me if I do it.

Actually, you need to step back in time with me a few years, to a day when I was having a conversation with God. But please don't be fooled. This wasn't the reverent, quiet-time variety to which I was just referring. No, no, no. This was the pitiful, excuse-filled, whiney, I-don't-have-time-to-do-everything, God,-don't-you-understand conversation. It went something like this: "What do You mean, I should spend regular time talking to You? I mean, I know You're right, like um…You're…You know… God. But have You seen my life? *Regular* is not a word that applies. There is *nothing* that I do on a consistent basis in my day. I have a one-year-old. My life has no routine to it."

> **"There is nothing that I do on a consistent basis in my day. I have a one-year-old. My life has no routine to it."**

And then, in that gentle but clear way that only God can speak, He reminded me of my habit. I use the word *habit* rather loosely. Some people are connoisseurs of coffee. I am an addict. I really *need* my morning coffee. It doesn't even have to be particularly good coffee. It just needs to be available within fifteen minutes or so of my rising. There it was…a habit…a routine. And I certainly couldn't argue that time with God was not as important as that java moment that started each of my days. I was convicted. So my habit changed.

Now, before I could put that much-anticipated steaming cup of coffee to my lips, I had to be in my chair, have my Bible open, have my study open, have my pen next to me, and be ready to share the opening moments of my day with someone who had been missing me, my Savior. That was about two years ago. And my morning quiet time is now a part of me. It's as regular as the sunrise.

The moral of the story is, if you can tie your devotions to an addiction, you're in there!!!! No, no, no. That's not it. What I really want to say is that some amazing and unexpected gifts came from this single act of obedience. Certainly I grew in knowledge and faith and love for my God. But here's the surprise. My son began slipping into the room while I studied or prayed. He would scrunch his skinny frame in next to me in the medium-sized stuffed chair. And he would just sit there. This didn't happen just once or twice but frequently. When I pressed him on what drew him in, he finally articulated that he just wanted to be near me *when I was still*. He never got to be around me when I was quiet and calm and reverent and at peace. And he wanted a piece of me when I, finally, was all those things. I never pushed him to join in my study. But sometimes I would tell him something that really struck me in my readings. We've had some of the most incredible conversations during these special morning times.

A friend of mine gave me a valuable insight when I told her about this experience with my son. She said a bigger lesson, which I probably didn't even realize I was teaching, was about submitting to authority. How could I ask my son to stand still before *me*, listen respectfully to *me*, come when I called him to *me*, if it was clear to him that I wasn't doing those same things before my God, *my* authority? I would have completely lacked any credibility. What other lessons am I teaching without knowing it? As Emerson reminds us, "The years teach us much the days never knew."

Find a Perspective That Steps Above the Fray

This is a harder one to communicate. It's about looking at *something* differently. This thing, whatever it is, may often be the source of great frustration or even misery for you. But with a simple change in perspective, the way you feel about it is radically altered. Absolutely nothing else changes.

I once read of a woman who hated sorting the laundry. She actually loathed it and found herself to be angry and bitter whenever called to this repetitive and endless task. At one point in her frustration she was folding a frilly, lace-covered girl's outfit. She was reminded of all the years that she had folded only boy things and how she and her husband had longed for a little girl in their family. This tearful moment became her laundry epiphany. Each folded item became a prayer-felt "thank you" that she was blessed with this child in her family. I don't know that she forever danced joyfully into the laundry room, but she did have this place in her mind to go when she needed recentering, when she needed to step above the fray.

I've had a similar revelation regarding the noise and disorder in my home. We are not a quiet family. We laugh loudly. We joke loudly. We tease loudly. We sing out in sudden silliness. We jump out from behind couches and say, "Boo." Sometimes, just sometimes, my cup of noise capacity overflows. I react strongly to the noise and the general chaos. I complain about how I shouldn't even bother cleaning up because "they'll just go around behind me and mess it all up again." I can become wrapped up in anger at the treadmill feeling of my existence. I find that I sometimes long for a bit of the quiet, contemplative moments I regularly experienced before I had children.

And then one day I was struck with the thought that one drunk driver could cross over into our lane of traffic and tragically I could lose all those sounds and the chaos in my life. Wouldn't I then find myself alone in a neatly ordered house, looking at a drawer of clothes that never needs straightening, staring at toys that no longer come out of their toy box, desperately wishing to hear all that noise just once more? And wouldn't I just want to die? Aren't there couples all over America who are praying for fingerprints all over their kitchen or drawings on their walls or children's dirty plates in their sinks? Sometimes we just need to focus on the exact same experience with a new lens. We need to be reminded that every gift comes with responsibilities and that every responsibility comes with a gift. If we only see the work, we've missed the best part.

> **We need to be reminded that every gift comes with responsibilities and that every responsibility comes with a gift. If we only see the work, we've missed the best part.**

If you find yourself truly at odds with something in your life, step back for a moment and see if you can't find a new lens, one that finds the gifts in your circumstances instead of all the challenges. Aren't you glad that this is exactly how God sees us?

Making these radical changes means questioning everything you do, every use of your time, every expenditure of your resources, even the way you think. It isn't easy to do, and it might be uncomfortable. It's much easier to just accept what our culture says should be on our plate. It's much easier to just step on to the ever moving treadmill and let it carry us along. It's much easier not to stand out in the crowd for choosing a different path. But if we're tired of always running, if we're not sure what we're running to, and what we're running from, a little temporary discomfort is worth the deep sense of restoration that a little—or a lot—of margin in our lives will ultimately bring.

Endnote

1. Amy Dacyczyn, *The Complete Tightwad Gazette* (New York: Villard Books, 1998).

Chapter 8

Awareness Statement #8:

We Are Not Defective

I see her coming down the hall of the large facility in which our annual state homeschool convention takes place. Peaceful Patty or Godly Gladys or maybe Efficient Ethel. She's one and the same. She is so very ordered. So calm. Her children are in a perfect line behind her like little *Sound of Music* stairstep kids. *They* are respectful. *They* are quiet. *They* are color coordinated.

She likewise sees me coming from the other end of the hall. Even from this distance she can recognize me. Is it the ever-present, huge catchall bag falling off of my shoulder? Is it the wet stain on the front of my shirt from my freshly spilled coffee? Maybe it's the armload of books and papers shoved askew into a hapless pile in my arms. My children are behind me as well…somewhere…in the nearby crowd.

We meet and greet generally in the middle. As we chat, another friend stops by briefly and asks if one of us has a pen. I begin to pat furiously at my hair as though a small fire has possibly erupted and must be quickly extinguished lest it engulf my entire head. Huh, that's funny, no pen. Usually two or three are either residing behind my ear or resting in the topknot that sometimes passes as an attempt to do my hair.

While I continue my patting frenzy, Organized Olivia swoops her hand backward in one Olympic-worthy arcing motion, slips it into her neatly ordered bag, retrieves a lovely pen, clicks the internal workings into place on the return arc, and hands the pen to the friend while maintaining eye contact and quoting scripture.

In my heart of hearts, I worry that she's judging me. I see that sweet smile on her face that leaves me thinking she's wondering how I'm even going to find my car in the parking lot later. (She is apparently unaware of the feather-topped toilet plunger firmly affixed to the roof of my car for just such purposes.) I even secretly believe she might think that my relationship with God is in question. Surely, she speculates, I don't even pause long enough to hear the quiet voice of God in my day. And for quite some time, years even, I wondered right along with her.

Do you know this woman? I do. Several of them in fact. And they are lovely people to boot! There really is an enviable quality to women who orchestrate such calm and order in their families. It is almost tempting to believe that I should be just like them. They get a great many positive strokes in our culture, even more in our church culture, for just such qualities. I could almost come away believing that my qualities, indeed any qualities other than what I see in them, are defective. But to do so would be to miss the gifts that God gave to me. Struggling to obtain their innate sense of order would leave me defeated as I attempt a state that I cannot achieve and, in the process, would cause me to lose a precious state for which I am perfectly designed.

> **Mary chose to absorb the moment, to fill her mind with the gifts Christ brought to her, to set aside the maintenance of life for the beauty of the moment.**

You and I, we unregimented moms, also are praiseworthy. We really are. But if your focus has been on others, chances are you haven't seen the gifts God has placed in you. If you've been so busy trying to remove perceived deficits, you have probably never really found the qualities that make you shine. And you certainly haven't fulfilled your unique role in His kingdom. I'm not denying that there is a downside to our non-linear nature. Being highly unregimented does bring real organizational challenges with it, I'll admit. But it also comes with a wonderful upside, if you can learn to stop suppressing your unregimented side, and if you can stop pretending that you're supposed to be one of those live-to-organize moms, if you can learn to have fun with the way your mind works. YOU can create a delightful home for your family.

Liberating Insight from Mary and Martha

The world gives so much support to the highly organized and industrious woman. But Jesus offered a different spin worth investigating. Take a look at the Bible's passage

(Luke 10:38–42) about Mary and Martha. Luke tells us that Martha "opened her home" to Jesus when He visited. Sounds good, right? She set herself about doing the "preparations that had to be made." Since they needed to be made and she went about doing them, that also sounds good. But Mary, she doesn't help with the preparations at all. Mary just flops herself down at Jesus' feet and listens. Martha is indignant and complains to Jesus of Mary's disregard for all the work to be done.

Jesus then stuns Martha by saying, "Mary has chosen what is better." Did you catch that? Mary, who let the housework go and permitted herself the indulgence of the moment, had chosen the better. And why was it better? Take hold of this truth. Christ said, "Mary has chosen what is better, and *it will not be taken away from her*" (emphasis mine). Mary chose to absorb the moment, to fill her mind with the gifts Christ brought to her, to set aside the maintenance of life for the beauty of the moment. When next month rolled around, Martha's cleaned linens and beautiful meal would be gone, taken from her by time and the continuing march of life. But Mary's experience and wisdom and growing faith would still be there. It *will not be taken from her*, and it will serve her for an eternity.

Herein lies a great lesson for us. The first obvious insight that we must be careful not to miss is that both types of women are needed. This is essential to understand. That organized woman? That Martha?? She is the one who sees to maintenance details. She sees to it that Jesus gets fed. She sees to it that the bed linens are laid out so that He'll have a place to sleep that night. She gets busy planning and executing a splendid meal for this honored guest. And that's important. But for all of her great attention to detail, Martha's downside is that she misses some jewels of the moment. Only a Martha could walk with Jesus toward the grave of her very dead brother, feel the energy in the air as something wondrous is about to happen, sense the building excitement as Jesus commands the gravestone to be moved, yet miss the jewel of the moment by making her famous proclamation,

We also need to give ourselves permission to be Mary, to ride out the wave of the moment of wonder.

"But Lord, by now he shall surely stinketh" (Carol translation). She is so painstakingly focused on the details of things to be done that the energy and delight of the moment can be totally lost on her.

Martha and Mary are often seen in contrast to each other. We know that Martha busied herself looking after things. I have this picture in my mind of Mary staring into the eyes of Jesus, her chin resting in her hand, her elbow on the table, while Martha sits upright, also at the table. A disciple accidentally tips over a cup, spilling its contents on the table before them. Mary nonchalantly reaches for a towel and mindlessly begins to sop up the mess while keeping her gaze on Jesus and staying focused on His story. Martha, however, has swooped from the room and returns with a rag, a bucket, and some stone table polish and sets about clucking around the table complaining about the possibility of a stain. While Martha was masterful at keeping things, sometimes the things were keeping Martha.

Mary didn't have the same gifts. While dusting around a window, she may have caught sight of a sunset or bird that kept her rapt attention for thirty minutes, leaving the dusting unfinished (minutes wasted, in Martha's opinion). Mary's room probably wasn't always as neat as Martha's. Perhaps Mary hastily tossed her bedroll into the corner as she ran out to visit with a neighbor. Possibly she had to pull away a small plate of grapes and olives that she had left on the chair before Jesus could even sit down when He visited. She may have begged Jesus to tell her a parable without first remembering to offer Him a drink. All of that's quite possible. But…she was THERE, seizing the moment. She allowed herself to get swept away in the wonderful. Jesus' words now harken back to us.

We are Marys, not Marthas. And while we need to borrow some of Martha's habits just to keep a bit of organization in our life, I think we also need to give ourselves permission to be Mary, to ride out the wave of the moment of wonder. Consider with me some of the advantages, the blessings, that being a Mary brings.

Able to Think Outside the Box

We unregimented moms are not rigid in our thinking. Frankly, we kind of like letting our minds meander, popping around here and there. Our nonlinear, flowing thoughts allow us to more easily think outside the box. Indeed, the walls of the box don't even form a clear square in our minds. This is an often missed but a highly valuable gift. Because of this, we are good problem solvers. We can think of possible solutions that would never have emerged from a more structured mind. Now remember, we need the ordered mom. She will probably be better able to execute our idea once she envisions it, because she will realize all the details that will need to be addressed to assure its success. But the seed of that great idea is more likely to emerge from the mind that thinks out of the box.

> **If you can instill in your children a love of the unexplored and a total dismissal of the fear of failure, you have empowered them for life.**

Our one mistake here is that we like to think out loud. So while we're letting our mind meander through a zillion solutions (five-sixths of which even we agree are preposterous), we have now laid bare to the listening world just how bizarrely structured our thought processes really are. Not pretty. Perhaps better to save the out-loud part for the final solution.

The La-Di-Da Factor

Since we like new ideas, and indeed are struck with new ideas (or is that distractions?) at the rate of about seven per minute, we have probably tried many new ideas. If truth be told, we might even be termed "impulsive" (although I am much more partial to "spontaneous"). And since all new ideas have a higher failure rate than old ideas, we're kind of used to things not always working out. We develop an almost "la-di-da" mentality about failure, and the treasure in that attitude is that we aren't destroyed or paralyzed by our failure. Failure becomes a concept that is almost meaningless other than for its ability to point us to another, yet untried solution.

Now here's the treasure, the gift to our family: if you can instill in your children a love of the unexplored and a total dismissal of the fear of failure, you have empowered them for life. Think about it. What researcher doesn't need this combination of skills? What designer? What inventor? Thomas Edison tested over three thousand different theories in his development of the lightbulb. If he fell apart after his first failure, we wouldn't have this culture-changing invention.

> **Conversations with those of us who are not straightforward in our thought processes are an adventure.**

How many of today's adults are hindered by their own lack of this quality? How many would like to apply for a different job but freeze at the idea of moving to a new location? How many would like to sing in church, talk to a visitor, vacation in an exotic country, wear something different, speak in public, go back to school, ask a difficult question of a boss, try *anything* new?

We unregimented moms share with our children a glorious sense of la-di-da that can free them to achieve all that they can dream. See this for the very real gift that it is.

Delight-Driven Conversation

People who are linear in their thinking have a thought, speak the thought, complete the thought, and they're done. Nothing is left out. Nothing is added. On the other hand, conversations with those of us who are not straightforward in our thought processes are an adventure. I believe that I personally have elevated nonlinear thinking to an art form. I will pop up with some thought or idea that will have no seeming connection to the previous statements. But if you had the time, I could take you through the twenty-seven steps that took me from there to here. The plus side to conversing with a nonlinear thinker is that the conversation tends to be driven by whatever delights, enthralls, or impacts the speaker for the moment. Nonlinear thinkers are usually quite enthusiastic about whatever topic they are discussing. Although their conversation may be a bit disjointed, it is usually, nonetheless, quite interesting.

Delight-Driven Homeschooling

In the same vein, homeschooling can be delight driven. Think back with me to high school. Do you recall any of your classes that were especially dull? Did you ever have any teachers who presented the course information, successfully covered the material, yes, and made it from point A to point B, but were so obviously bored by their own subject matter that they themselves seemed at risk of nodding off? Can you imagine that same class taught by someone who was enthralled by the subject matter, someone who had just read something last month that had sparked an in-depth search for material that further moti-

Knowing how to shift gears easily and joyfully is a real gift and can be a great blessing to your family.

vated his or her interest? That is exactly what our children often get from us if we allow ourselves the freedom to pursue our sudden interests. Information presented to kids in this manner is always relevant. It is always connected to something neat that they've just heard or seen, and the desire to know more is immediate. Furthermore, without even trying, presenting information in such a way teaches the unspoken lesson that

learning is fun and exciting. It teaches how to research and follow up on desired information. It teaches that information isn't to be spoon-fed to a robotic and dreary student but rather is to be attacked, discovered, and pursued with delight. It teaches an enthusiasm for life and study. What a gift to give our children.

The True Value in a Home

The home of a gloriously unregimented mom will probably have more disorder in it than other homes. We've already acknowledged that. But in this there resides a very beautiful, quiet gift that we might miss. We are not tied to things. I have been in homes that are full of absolutely beautiful things. These houses are lovely to look upon, but sometimes I get the feeling that the look of the home is more important than the life that occurs inside the home. Sometimes it seems that the *things* are given more care and accommodation than the people. To give these folks the benefit of the doubt, that order is probably the very thing that does relax them. They need to maintain that order for themselves, and since they believe it is essential to everyone's sense of calm, they are driven to maintain it for their guests as well. But sometimes their level of discomfort over anything that falls outside of their plan of organization brings a strain and stress to the visit that is not at all welcoming.

I will admit that from time to time I have longed for a bit more order in my home (or at least my husband has). But the blessing I have given my family here is the clear knowledge that they are more important to me than my things. If a glass is broken, it is not a crisis. If a spill occurs, we simply clean it up. We live in a house that I hope people will want to visit, a house in which they can relax and feel cherished for their presence and their laughter.

Easy Shifting

Since our minds are constantly trying out new directions, we are never rigorously tied to any plan. Changes of plans delight us. New things to see, places to go, people to meet.

The clear benefit to this is that when life happens and plans unexpectedly change, we don't fall apart. We adjust sooner and more quickly than others. We waste little time mourning the loss of the original plan. And we are the first to start getting excited about the possibilities that could arise from a new plan. We are the ones who can reinflate our glum and depressed family members who may have a hard time shifting gears. Again, let's acknowledge that we need our family's focused and dogged determination once a new plan of attack has been established. But during the sometimes painful process of shifting gears through one of the many inevitable and sudden changes that life presents, we are the oil that greases those gears. We make for easier transitions. We help diminish the tension and retrieve the joy. Knowing how to shift gears easily and joyfully is a real gift and can be a great blessing to your family.

Color and Eccentricity

Finally, I believe that the unregimented souls of this world are simply more colorful. I sense a greater expressiveness in their communications, more enthusiasm in their actions, a joy in their experience of life. The unregimented mom provides a lightness, a casual, relaxed atmosphere, an airiness (not airheadedness, thank you) that makes her infinitely more accessible and even appealing. A few of us are so colorful as to be eccentric, but that, too, has a gift attached. Eccentric is rarely boring. It may be many other things, but it is usually worth the price of admission just for the entertainment value.

The greatest gift here, however, is in teaching your children to be content with being different, to even revel in it, celebrate it, grow comfortable in it, and be able to laugh with it. I guarantee you, there will be a time when your children will

> **Your children were placed in your home by a wise and all-loving God who knew what He was doing.**

each be in a situation in which their expression of their faith will make them the odd one out. They will be in situations where they *are* different from everyone else. In fact, that's the call of Christianity—to be set apart, different, comfortably, even proudly so, and ready to do the will of God.

I once heard of a mom who sat at the table with her children admonishing them to be neat in their eating. She noticed her son poise some peas on a spoon in launch mode, ready to plaster his sister. Something possessed her. She explained to her son that he shouldn't hold peas like that, demonstrating with her own spoon, while explaining that even in jest his finger could slip and there would be a mess. He looked at her with that admonished look of resignation. And then…she let the peas fly. This boy was so stunned he couldn't respond, at least not for two and a half seconds, giving her time to reload. Soon the peas were flying all over. The baby was giggling, and the boy was laughing hysterically under the table to avoid mom's deadly accurate, reloaded spoon.

Okay, I'll admit it. That mom was me. And I will also acknowledge that we were finding peas for a week. But what a memory! The day of the "Pea Wars." We never repeated it. We didn't have to. It was relived in our laughter many times over. I'm not saying that you want to develop a disregard for manners in your children or cultivate a disrespect for property. But it wouldn't hurt to occasionally follow our urge for spontaneity. It's the delightful part of us that balances out our lack of natural orderliness. And it's high time we developed it.

I am so convinced that God has a plan for us that includes our Mary-like qualities. We all recognize the plan for the Marthas. We're regularly reminded of all they can get done. But if we try to be like them, we miss the plan for the Marys, for us. Run with this model. Borrow from Martha and organize to live where you need to. Fine. But there is a delight-driven, Mary-part of you that is at its very best when being spontaneous. Your children were placed in your home by a wise and all-loving God who knew what He was doing. There is something your children are supposed to absorb from your love of life and spontaneity that they will need if they are to become what God has intended for them. You may be raising a serious Type A personality who will die of a heart attack at age thirty-seven unless he learns to laugh or learns to leave margin in his life. There are committees on which you might serve that could get mired down by their own administrative complexities unless they learn to find a bit more of the la-di-da side of life. And there are people to be reached for the kingdom who are tailor-made to be attracted to your spontaneous, casual, delight-filled ways.

Start listening to your impulses. Don't automatically dismiss them in order to stay on the well-ordered Martha plan. Some of your delight-driven meanderings will create memories for life. Seek out the ways that God can use you, just as you are, just as He designed you. Pray that He will enable you to get caught up in the wonderfulness of the many gifts He's placed in our world and in our lives. Fulfill this gift He has placed within you. And have a very Mary day.

Resources

Sign Language Alphabet

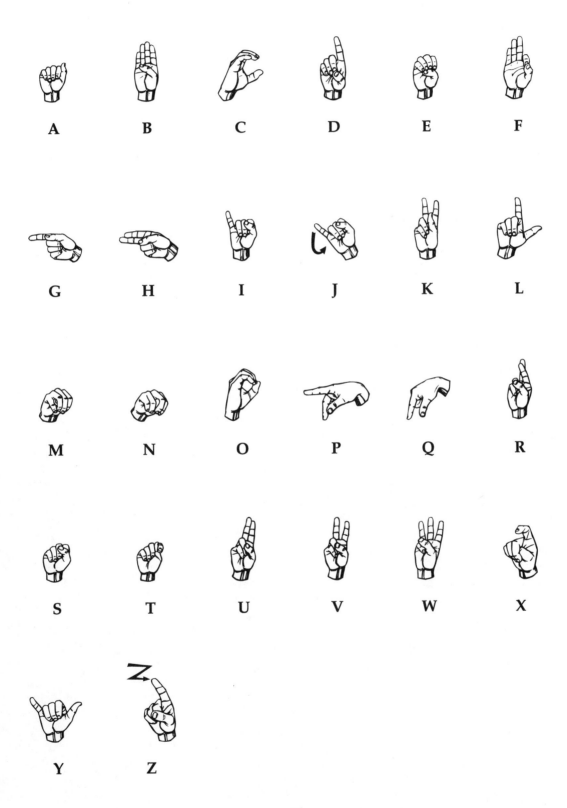

Family Night Pizza Dough

3½ C. flour
4 T. brown sugar
2 tsp salt
1 T. yeast
1 C. 120 degree water
1 T. olive oil

Mix water, oil, and yeast. Set aside for 10 minutes to "proof" your yeast.

Heat oven to 200 degrees and turn off immediately when 200 degrees is reached. This will make a perfect location for raising the dough.

Place flour, brown sugar, and salt into a food processor.

Add wet ingredients to dry in the food processor. Mix on low until a ball of dough forms. Add flour or water as needed to make a ball that wipes the sides of the food processor clean. Turn up to medium and allow ball to rotate around the bowl approximately 25 times. (You can mix and knead by hand. But a food processor is one of the best and most rapid kneaders of dough you'll ever find.)

Place the dough ball into a greased bowl, set into warm oven, and let rise for 45 minutes to an hour, or until doubled in size.

Remove dough and stretch to desired size for your pizza. Bake at 450 degrees.

Fine Tuning for Fabulous Pizza

- We stretch this pizza dough out to a large size of about 18 inches diameter. But if you want a thicker crust, stretch it less.
- Pre-bake your crust at 450 degrees for about 7–8 minutes. It should barely be beginning to brown when you remove it. This will alleviate the soggy center you often find in homemade pizzas.
- Our family likes a seasoned crust. So I spray the edges with a coating of vegetable spray and then coat lightly with a garlic powder, steak salt, and other spices. The smell of this baking will bring them all to the table.
- We use plain old spaghetti sauce for our pizza sauce. It's almost always available in our pantry and often costs less than jars of pizza sauce. Then top with shredded mozzarella cheese and your favorite toppings.
- Finally, bake a second time, again for about 7–8 minutes or until toppings have reached desired softness.

Seriously Yummy Microwave Caramel Corn

2 12-oz. bags of microwave popcorn
1 stick butter
1 C. brown sugar
¼ C. light corn syrup
½ tsp. salt
½ tsp. baking soda

Pop popcorn according to directions. Set aside.

Put next four ingredients into a microwave-safe bowl and heat in microwave until butter melts.

Stir well.

Put back in microwave for about 2½ minutes.

Add baking soda to mixture. Stir. Mixture will foam as soda reacts with ingredients.

Put popped corn into brown paper bag.

Pour hot mixture over the corn.

Close bag and shake well, evenly coating the popcorn with the caramel mixture.

Put bag in microwave and heat an additional 1½ minutes.

Allow to cool a bit. Then eat warm or spread in cake pan to cool.

Preschool Activities with Siblings

Arts and Crafts

- Create a greeting card to be sent to a grandparent, other relative, or friend.
- Create a play dough or other gooey concoction.
- Make paper dolls, paper Bible characters, or paper soldiers.
- Just color together.

Physical Activities: Gross Motor and Fine Motor

- Create a safe and fun obstacle course with pillows to jump over and circles on the floor made of masking tape in which the child stands while touching his or her toes or turning around, etc.
- Throw a beanbag back and forth.
- Throw a beanbag up, clap once, and catch.
- Place masking tape on the floor and have the child walk on the tape without losing his or her balance or stepping off.
- Teach the child to do jumping jacks. This takes more coordination than you might think.
- Teach one or two letters by asking the preschooler to shape his or her body like the letter. Don't introduce too many letters at one time.
- Practice "sewing" with a needle made of finely wound paper, taped into place. Then attach some yarn, also with tape. The child can "sew" through holes made into cardboard pieces shaped like animals or other recognizable objects.

Imagination Play

- Play out whatever situation the child wants. Perhaps it's supermarket, in which the sibling is a customer coming to buy things from the child. Perhaps it's just a tea party. Perhaps it's school. The important thing for the older sibling to remember is that the younger child—not the older sibling—is directing the activity.
- Put on a play for the family that acts out an event or story familiar to the child.

Life Skills

- Practice tying shoes, using visual language such as "Make two bunny ears. Make an 'X', and put one under. Pull, repeat!"
- Developing the fine motor skills needed to hold a pencil can be encouraged by making a prepared path. Draw a little creature at the entrance to a "road" that

101

meanders along until it finally ends with some destination reward. For example, a bee may be at the entrance to a road that leads to a flower or a pot of honey. Encourage the child to use a pencil to "travel" the road to the reward. See the sample on page 105.

- Make "ice cream" by putting milk and sugar to taste in a sandwich-sized ziplock baggie. Place this smaller baggie inside a gallon-sized baggie half full of crushed ice. Add some salt to the ice. Seal the outer bag. Now shake and shake and shake and shake. About ten minutes (or more) later, the inner bag will have soft-serve ice cream ready to be topped with your favorite ice-cream treats and eaten. Portions and baggies can be downsized for smaller hands and shorter times.

- Practice washing dishes. Expect some minor splashing and remaining puddles here. But kids love getting their hands into the water.

Read Books

- Reading to a younger sibling can be a launching point for other activities. For example, if you read the book *Ping* to the child, then the imagination play could be to act out the ducks leaving the boat, eating, and then returning. The physical activity could be to play Hide and Seek, since Ping hid from his master. For counting, the child could simply count the number of ducks he or she sees on a given page. For a craft the child could glue feathers onto a cutout of a duck. And so on.

- While reading a story to the child, pause and ask what he or she thinks might happen next. There is no right or wrong answer. The goal is simply to get the child thinking and more involved in the story.

- Have the child learn the poem "There Was an Old Lady Who Swallowed a Fly." Make an old lady out of household materials, such as plastic containers and cardboard. Be sure she has a mouth into which the animals can be fed (see drawing on page 104). Use toys or construction paper cut-outs to represent the animals in the poem (fly, spider, bird, cat, and so on). Encourage the child to put the animals in at just the right time while one of you recites the poem.

Counting and Numbers

- Play with blocks. Encourage counting when the child is open to it.
- Play a simple board game that encourages basic counting. We like Snail's Pace Race by Ravensburger.
- Give the child a stack of pennies and five cups with the numbers, 1, 2, 3, 4, and 5 on each cup respectively. Then encourage the child to put the correct number of pennies into each cup.

Thinking Games

- Using construction paper or foam paper, make two sets of an animal of your choice with very simple parts. Our two bunnies have a body, a head, two ears, a fluffy tail, and a bow tie. Create a bunny from one set of parts. Encourage the child to create a duplicate. Or create two bunnies, making only one thing different. See if the child can determine "what's missing."
- Play Old Maid.
- Copy down the preschooler's knock-knock jokes, and read them back to him or her with much laughter, no matter how silly they are.

Musical Activities

- Any number of songs with motions are available in books. We really like the "Wee Sing" book and CD.
- Create an "orchestra" from the various stuffed animals in your collection. Put on a great piece of music and allow the child to "direct" the orchestra.

Note: This is by no means an exhaustive list; it is simply a starting point. If you would like your older children to keep track of the activities they do with their younger siblings, use the handy reproducible Preschool Program form on page 107.

The Old Lady Who Swallowed a Fly

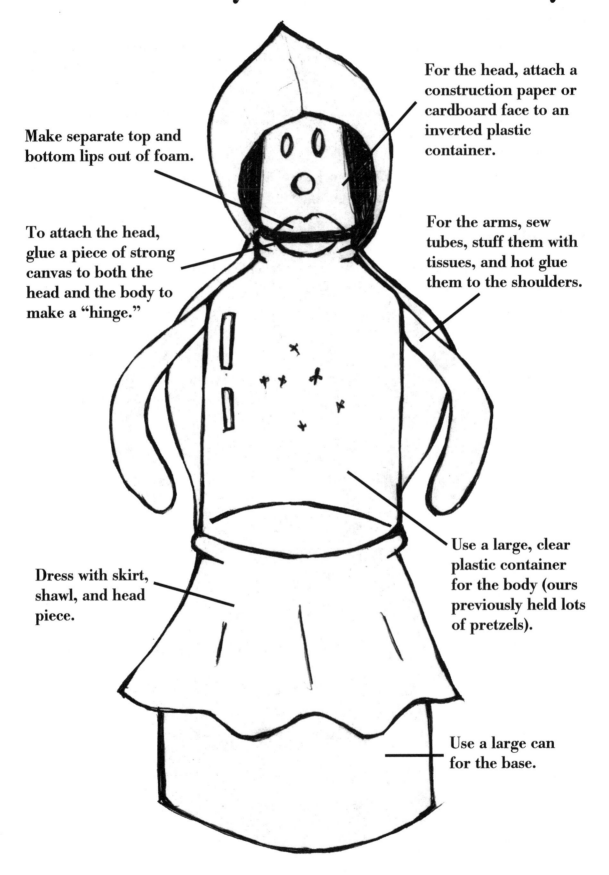

For the head, attach a construction paper or cardboard face to an inverted plastic container.

Make separate top and bottom lips out of foam.

To attach the head, glue a piece of strong canvas to both the head and the body to make a "hinge."

For the arms, sew tubes, stuff them with tissues, and hot glue them to the shoulders.

Use a large, clear plastic container for the body (ours previously held lots of pretzels).

Dress with skirt, shawl, and head piece.

Use a large can for the base.

Preschool Program

Date _____

Diaper Changes _____

Food Taken _____

_____

Sibling _____ Preschooler _____

Under each activity type, record what you did with the preschooler.

Arts and Crafts

Physical Activities

Imagination Play

Life Skills

Books Read

Counting / Numbers

Thinking Games

Musical Activities

A Starter List for "Boredom Day"

These are just a few ideas to get you started. Books and the Internet provide thousands more. I highly recommend *The Stuff That Fun Is Made Of* by Selena LaPorte.[1] Her book is full of easy recipes for homemade paints, play doughs, and just about everything else.

- Make butterflies. First, lay out paper on the floor. Then, using poster paints, paint a beautiful design on the bottoms of your feet. Work quickly before the paint dries. Next, make a print with each foot by stepping on the paper; be sure to step your left foot to the right and then your right foot to the left, keeping them apart by about an inch. Using black paint, add an elongated body in the center and two antennae coming off the top. The result is pretty remarkable. We've kept our butterflies for years!
- Create a comic strip.
- Make a fort with sheets, blankets, and couch cushions.
- Learn to crochet.
- Create a web page for yourself or your family.
- Trace your body on a large sheet of paper. Color in your clothes and face.
- Make a list of animals, one for each letter of the alphabet.
- Create a backyard "Olympics," with broad jump, across-the-yard dash, Frisbee throw, etc. Award paper gold, silver, and bronze medals.
- Memorize a poem or Bible verse.
- Write a letter to a friend or grandparent.
- Write an autobiography.
- Call and interview an older family relative. Record or write down his or her stories for safekeeping.
- Play beanbag golf. Place boxes at different spots in the yard or basement. Number them. Keeping one foot in the first box, throw a beanbag toward the next box. Then, keeping a foot where the beanbag landed, throw the beanbag again. Estimate par for each box. Tally "strokes" for "hole." Play several rounds.
- Do a crossword puzzle.
- Put twenty things on a tray. Look at them. Cover them. See how many you can list from memory.
- Create a miniature kingdom for imaginary Bug Royalty. Use moss for carpet, leaves and twigs for furniture, flowers for adornments.
- Create a "peek under the flap" book.
- Learn the sign language alphabet.

- Create Switcheroos. Changing the beginning letter or sound of one word and replacing with another letter or sound results in a different but rhyming word. You provide two clues, and your playmate figures it out. Example: What starts as something a horse pulls and ends up as being very clever? Answer: Cart - Smart.
- Create parachutes with hankies (does anyone still have these?) or with cut-up garbage-can liners, and launch a small nonbreakable object. See if you can increase the time that objects remain airborne.
- Open a lemonade stand.
- Make bird feeders. Tie a string around a pine cone in such a way that it will hang nicely. Then coat it with peanut butter and roll it in birdseed.
- Create puppets and put on a show.
- Learn to play Cats' Cradles with string.
- Create a limerick.
- Make your own wrapping paper by making a potato stamp and stamping a design on some large sheets of paper.
- If you've got a basketball hoop, shoot the ball till you've made one hundred baskets.
- Create a miniature golf course in your house. Make stand-up animals, buildings, or other designs. A "hole" is scored by getting the ball through the legs of the animal or through an open door in the building. Make a club by attaching cardboard as a "head" to the base of a ruler. The balls can be ping pong balls or even tightly wadded up aluminum foil.
- Sew something.
- Gather many different types of seeds. Outline a basic picture. Using the seeds, create a mosaic. Or simply use small, cut-up squares of colorful construction paper. Putting the design on a black background makes for a beautiful effect.

Endnote

1. Selena LaPorte, *The Stuff That Fun Is Made Of* (Lynnwood: Emerald Books, 2001).

Carol Barnier

A popular speaker who has shared her message of encouragement at conferences and on radio shows around the country, Carol provides highly practical suggestions and thought-provoking insight all wrapped up in a package that leaves you laughing. A great speaker for anyone who has ever asked the questions:

- Why am I made this way?
- Why are my children made that way?
- Why does life happen this way?

We all love gifts from God. At least we love them when they're what we've always hoped for and wanted. But Carol Barnier believes that we miss many of God's greatest gifts in ourselves and in our children because we fail to truly OPEN THE GIFTS.

In the case of our children, we're much more likely to take the gift of a child and place him or her on a shelf to admire and to compare to all the children God has given to others. We want this gift box of ours to take on the shape we've seen in others, something familiar, something typical. We're uncomfortable when our gift box isn't quite like all the others—when this child doesn't act, think, or learn like other children. In the case of ourselves, we want our gifts to look exactly like the gifts we see in other women. We don't want our uniqueness to shine through. We don't want our differences to be noticed. But in taking these approaches, we often step off the plan for which God designed us.

Carol encourages her audience to see that these differences ARE gifts…and to plunge into the delicious process of opening the gifts sent to us by our heavenly Father, learning to use our uniqueness to live out the wondrous plan made on our behalf.

Interested in having Carol as a possible speaker for your next event? Contact her by clicking on "Booking Information" at

www.OpenGifts.org

Carol Barnier is also the author of *How to Get Your Child off the Refrigerator and on to Learning: Homeschooling Highly Distractible, ADHD, or Just Plain Fidgety Kids*, also published by Emerald Books.